"In this penetrating and sophisticated critique, Brown challenges relational thinkers to examine the ways in which their understanding of metapsychology has resulted in retaining an overly narrow and restrictive set of relational values that betray an underlying commitment to philosophical materialism. Although founded on pluralism and critical eclecticism, relational theory continues to marginalize other approaches such as the Jungian and transpersonal schools. This subtle philosophical study will be of interest to all those interested in the implications of relational theory and spirituality."

–Lewis Aron, Ph.D, ABPP, Director of the New York University Postdoctoral Program in Psychotherapy & Psychoanalysis, and past-President of the Division of Psychoanalysis (39) of the APA.

"Freud himself, and psychoanalysis following him for most of the last century, eschewed religion and embraced a materialistic and even positivistic vision of psychoanalysis as an objective science. Recent decades have begun to witness a renewed openness to dialogue between spiritual and psychoanalytic practice, even allowing for the recognition of psychoanalysis itself as a sacred practice. Robin S. Brown provides a thorough and challenging investigation of the mutual fitting together of psychoanalysis and spirituality."

–Galit Atlas, Ph.D, author of *The Enigma of Desire: Sex Longing and Belonging in Psychoanalysis.*

"A powerful, incisive critical analysis of the state of contemporary psychoanalysis. Robin S. Brown persuades with passionate intelligence for a return to first principles as the basis for a much needed, broader, more inclusive approach to the psyche. A welcome new voice on the analytic scene."

–Joe Cambray, Ph.D, Provost at Pacifica Graduate Institute, past-President of the International Association for Analytical Psychology, and author of *Synchronicity: Nature and Psyche in an Interconnected Universe.*

"Scholarly, rigorous, and theoretically sophisticated, Robin S. Brown's *Psychoanalysis Beyond the End of Metaphysics* is a groundbreaking application of participatory thinking to contemporary psychoanalysis—one that leads to the emergence of a novel post-relational approach to psychoanalytic theory and practice. Brown shows how contemporary psychoanalysis can embrace a creative pluralism capable of successfully navigating between both metaphysical certainties and the exhausted relativisms of postmodernity."

–Jorge Ferrer, Ph.D, Professor of East-West psychology with the California Institute of Integral Studies, and author of *Revisioning Transpersonal Theory: A Participatory Vision of Human Spirituality.*

"This book genuinely breaks new ground. Perhaps more accurately, Robin S. Brown has reimagined a grounding, a communal space, and a common ground in which individuality and relationality co-mingle. He argues that such a project, if genuinely to avoid the polarities that limit psychoanalysis in every direction, must be grounded in ethics and in faith. This daunting task seems at the same time absolutely necessary and this book makes a compelling and rigorous contribution to this project."

–Adrienne Harris, Ph.D, faculty and supervisor with the New York University Postdoctoral Program in Psychotherapy & Psychoanalysis, and author of *Gender as Soft Assembly*.

"Equipped with an impressive array of sources, philosophical ideas and traditions, including those of the philosophy of mind, metaphysics, and German idealism, Brown confidently exposes the limitations of some of the basic assumptions in relational theory and psychoanalytic practice. Rather than abandon such theories on this basis, Brown proffers a compelling argument to resituate them within a broader and more efficacious framework, one that reinforces the validity of the psychoanalytic profession and its capacity to incite social change. This work is a significant contribution to the debate about the value of psychoanalytic theory and practice today."

–Lucy Huskinson, Ph.D, School of Philosophy & Religion, Bangor University, UK, and co-Editor-in-Chief of the *International Journal of Jungian Studies*.

"Following the thread of contemporary psychoanalytic dialogues, Robin S. Brown, in a courageous, intelligent and nuanced manner, finds his way to the edges between different schools and perspectives of analytic thinking. Challenging yet respectful, Brown expands our psychoanalytic vision beyond orthodoxies and recovers margin-alized voices, neglected or repressed by the dominant traditions. Going beyond simple criticism, he articulates a creative, post-relational view of psychoanalysis, in touch with and grounded in philosophical foundations too often ignored or taken for granted in most schools of analysis. Those interested in the current thinking about psychoanalysis, from curious beginners to seasoned analysts and scholars, will find in this book an important, refreshing and challenging perspective."

–Stanton Marlan, Ph.D, ABPP, president of the Pittsburgh Society of Jungian Analysts, and senior clinical supervisor at Duquesne University.

"Brown points the way beyond decades of stagnation. He brings to the table an eclectic tonal range—from the history of German Idealism, to relational, Lacanian and Jungian psychoanalysis. Yes, you heard right—Jung! For those of us who have been dismissive of Jung, Brown's guidance shows us what a series of misapprehensions we have colluded in; how Jung's work might open up the eternally recurrent impasse between subjectivity and objectivity, as well as our ethical responsibility as clinicians to both the individual and the wider world."

–Jamieson Webster, Ph.D, adjunct faculty with the New School, and author of *The Life and Death of Psychoanalysis*.

PSYCHOANALYSIS BEYOND THE END OF METAPHYSICS

Psychoanalysis Beyond the End of Metaphysics offers a new paradigm approach which advocates reengaging the importance of metaphysics in psychoanalytic theorizing. The emergence of the relational trend has witnessed a revitalizing influx of new ideas, reflecting a fundamental commitment to the principle of dialogue. However, the transition towards a more pluralistic discourse remains a work in progress, and those schools of thought not directly associated with the relational shift continue to play only a marginal role.

In this book, Robin S. Brown argues that for contemporary psychoanalysis to more adequately reflect a clinical ethos of pluralism, the field must examine the extent to which a theoretical commitment to the notion of relationship can grow restrictive. Suggesting that in the very effort to negotiate theoretical biases, psychoanalytic practice may occlude a more adequate recognition of its own evolving assumptions, Brown proposes that the profession's advance requires a return to first principles. Arguing for the fundamental role played by faith in supporting the emergence of consciousness, this work situates itself at the crossroads of relational, Jungian, and transpersonal approaches to the psyche.

Psychoanalysis Beyond the End of Metaphysics will be of significant interest to all psychodynamically oriented clinicians, alongside scholars of depth psychology and the philosophy of mind. It will also be helpful to advanced and postgraduate students of psychoanalysis seeking to orient themselves in the field at present.

Robin S. Brown is a psychoanalytic clinician, and a member of adjunct faculty for the clinical psychology department at Teachers College, Columbia University. He lives and works in New York City.

PSYCHOANALYSIS BEYOND THE END OF METAPHYSICS

Thinking Towards the Post-Relational

Robin S. Brown

Routledge
Taylor & Francis Group

LONDON AND NEW YORK

First published 2017
by Routledge
2 Park Square, Milton Park, Abingdon, Oxon OX14 4RN

and by Routledge
711 Third Avenue, New York, NY 10017

Routledge is an imprint of the Taylor & Francis Group, an informa business

British Library Cataloguing in Publication Data
A catalogue record for this book is available from the British Library

Library of Congress Cataloging in Publication Data
Names: Brown, Robin S., author.
Title: Psychoanalysis beyond the end of metaphysics : thinking towards the post-relational / Robin S. Brown.
Description: Abingdon, Oxon ; New York, NY : Routledge, 2016. | Includes bibliographical references and index.
Identifiers: LCCN 2015047394| ISBN 9781138935174 (hardback) | ISBN 9781138935181 (pbk.)
Subjects: LCSH: Psychoanalysis and philosophy. | Metaphysics. | Psychoanalysis.
Classification: LCC BF175.4.P45 B767 2016 | DDC 150.19/5--dc23
LC record available at http://lccn.loc.gov/2015047394

ISBN: 978-1-138-93517-4 (hbk)
ISBN: 978-1-138-93518-1 (pbk)
ISBN: 978-1-315-67757-6 (ebk)

Typeset in Bembo
by Taylor & Francis Books

For Marie

CONTENTS

ACKNOWLEDGEMENTS

I would like to thank the faculty and staff of Blanton Peale Graduate Institute and Counseling Center for providing a supportive environment in which to work and learn. My appreciation goes to Nunzio Gubitosa, Joenine Roberts, Royce Froehlich, Jennifer Harper, Krystyna Sanderson, Lucinda Antrim, Lee Jenkins, Carol Triano, David Leeming, Shari K. Brink, Ann Springer, Supavadee Thaveesaengsiri, Diana Barone, Astha R. Bakhru Mootoo, Jane Roberts, Timothy Roberts, Ramesh Persaud, Karen Andre, Nancy Simpson, and Evril Boucher. In connection with the California Institute of Integral Studies, I would like to thank Connie Jones, Allan "Leslie" Combs, Keiron Le Grice, Jorge Ferrer, Alfonso Montuori, Daniel Deslauriers, Kathy Littles, and Martha Brumbaugh. At Routledge, I am most grateful to Kate Hawes for her faith in my work, and to Charles Bath for his assistance in steering through the publication process. Special thanks is reserved for the support offered by Aurelie Athan, Ashleigh Colin, Harry Fogarty, Michael O'Loughlin, and Lorna Peachin.

Passages occurring in Chapter 1 first appeared in a paper entitled "On the Significance of Psychodynamic Discourse for the Field of Consciousness Studies" which was published in *Consciousness: Ideas and Research for the Twenty First Century*. Sections of Chapter 3 and the book's coda appeared in a less worked-out form in an article entitled "Beyond the Evolutionary Paradigm in Consciousness Studies" which appeared in the *Journal of Transpersonal Psychology*. Part of the book's coda was originally published in an article entitled "On the Undisturbed Functioning of Memory" which featured in *Quadrant: the Journal of the C.G. Jung Foundation*. Thanks go respectively to editors Allan Combs, Marcie Boucouvalas, and Kathryn Madden for copyright permissions. The Edgar Morin epigraph appearing in the book's coda is reprinted with the kind permission of Hampton Press.

INTRODUCTION

Over the last thirty years, North American psychoanalysis has undergone a significant and necessary shift. In addition to offering new ways of thinking about the clinical situation, the relational movement has stimulated a broadening in psychoanalytic discourse. Because the relational turn has sought to question the notion of the analyst's authority, this ideal has been expressed in an approach to theoretical discourse that likewise strives towards mutual exchange. Thus relational thinking might be said to reflect two distinct tendencies: (1) a broad theoretical outlook emphasizing greater clinical openness engendering (2) a theoretical receptivity at the level of discourse itself which, if it is to be wholehearted, must allow for contrary positions that might even question the very basis upon which this receptivity is founded. In light of the complex challenges posed by the theme of diversity, however, it is important to acknowledge that this commitment to openness is itself founded in specific theoretical ideals. In this regard it might also be noted that in the relational movement's early history, the notion of theoretical inclusivity initially served quite unambiguously as a means to *opposing* classical thinking. The text generally understood to have inaugurated the relational shift, Greenberg and Mitchell's (1983) *Object Relations in Psychoanalytic Theory*, mobilizes a diversity of theoretical approaches under a banner of kinship so as to initiate a political shift in discourse that would seek to usurp the assumptions of mainstream thinking. From the outset, then, the relational movement's desire to draw different schools into conversation has, at least in part, served explicitly oppositional purposes. When Stephen Mitchell (1992) states in an early issue of *Psychoanalytic Dialogues*[1] that "the battle against orthodoxy has been largely won" (p. 443), it is notable that he adopts the kind of military metaphor typically associated with Freudian drive-theory, rather than the more dialogical tones usually encountered in relational discourse.

The following passage from Ghent (1992) is cited by Aron (1996) for its foundational significance in having launched the relational orientation associated with NYU's widely recognized postdoctoral program:

There is no such thing as a relational analyst; there are only analysts whose backgrounds may vary considerably, but who share a broad outlook in which human relations – specific, unique human relations – play a superordinate role in the genesis of character and of psychopathology, as well as in the practice of psychoanalytic therapeutics.

Relational theorists have in common an interest in the intrapsychic as well as the interpersonal, but the intrapsychic is seen as constituted largely by the internalization of interpersonal experience mediated by the constraints imposed by biologically organized templates and delimiters. Relational theorists tend also to share a view in which both reality and fantasy, both outer world and inner world, both the interpersonal and the intrapsychic, play immensely important and interactive roles in human life. Relational theorists do not substitute a naive environmentalism for drive theory. Due weight is given to what the individual brings to the interaction: temperament, bodily events, physiological responsivity, distinctive patterns of regulation, and sensitivity. Unlike earlier critics of drive theory, relational theorists do not minimize the importance of the body or of sexuality in human development. Relational theorists continue to be interested in the importance of conflict, although conflict most usually is seen as taking place between opposing relational configurations rather than between drive and defense. Relational theory is essentially a psychological, rather than a biological or quasi-biological theory; its primary concern is with issues of motivation and meaning and their vicissitudes in human development, psychopathology and treatment.

(Ghent, 1992, p. xviii)

Much can be made of this ambitious statement. The position outlined privileges human relationships yet wishes to accommodate the intrapsychic; focuses on the social without dismissing the significance of individual factors; and is avowedly psychological while nevertheless seeking to acknowledge the role of biology. The rhetorical strategy adopted here is not uncommon in relational discourse – it consists of establishing a dialectic between two seemingly opposed points of view and, while naturally privileging one side of the argument, nevertheless searching for a means to acknowledge both positions. Such an outlook reflects an open-ended accommodation to theoretical differences. Nevertheless, in its ostensible ambitions of inclusivity an approach of this kind may also subtly reflect an implicit belief that relational thinking "goes beyond" that which came before it, with this sense of going beyond figured precisely in having sought to accommodate opposing points of view. The idea of addressing both poles of the argument is misleading, however, in that the relational position nevertheless does admit to making certain theoretical commitments that privilege one side of the conversation. In having gone some way towards recognizing the importance of the opposing position, however, such an attitude potentially safeguards itself from the notion that something has been left out.

Considered dynamically, the affirmation of a given value is never without cost. The claims of relationship are therefore both a binding force, and an exclusionary one. Recognizing how the relational movement does indeed privilege certain theoretical commitments, Aron (1996) argues that this trend should be regarded as reflecting a necessary reaction to the biases of classical thinking: "Any tendency relational theory has to emphasize the superordinate position of a two-person psychology is predominantly as a corrective to classical psychoanalysis's focus on elements of a one-person psychology" (p. 62). Twenty years have passed since Aron made this well-justified statement. With the extent to which relational theorizing has since come to dominate North American psychoanalysis, however, the danger now emerges of a new form of one-sidedness. Perhaps in response to this threat, more recently Aron and Starr (2012) stress that the relational approach fundamentally reflects an effort to move beyond binaries, both in theory and in practice. This is a worthy intention, yet it raises the problem that we might confuse the relational ethos thus expressed with those commitments that first marked the movement's emergence. "Relational psychoanalysis" must by definition be considered a less inclusive designation than psychoanalysis per se. Aron and Starr write: "Polarization, like splitting, is a way of managing anxiety. It is not inherently pathological, but a necessary step in development. Anxiety discourages thirdness, a perspective from which binary oppositions can be broken down or deconstructed" (p. 30). While the endeavor to embrace thirdness is certainly admirable (not to mention historically lacking in psychoanalytic politics), the magnitude of the challenge thus implied is indicated by the fact that defining this position in itself establishes an opposition between splitting and thirdness. In this light, it might be emphasized that polarization doesn't only protect against anxiety, but also serves to clarify distinctions. Thus, just as thirdness follows polarization, polarization must follow thirdness. The challenge that Aron and Starr's reflections may therefore point to is in seeking to move fluidly between these positions without succumbing to the anxiety that can precipitate a fixation in *either* outlook.

In a noteworthy article, leading classical analyst Arnold Richards (2003) offers his own call for a dialectical approach to theoretical difference in preference to a discourse of "dichotomy and polarization" (p. 73). Ironically, in responding to this paper, the editors of *Psychoanalytic Dialogues* at the time, Altman and Davies (2003), accuse Richards of severely misrepresenting the relational school. They claim that Richards demeans relational thinking by portraying the movement as expressive of an underlying sense of victimization. Perhaps even more ironically, though, having dismissed the portrayal of relational thinking offered by Richards out of hand, Altman and Davies go on to prescribe a correct approach to "constructive dialogue" that entails a commitment to "mounting the best possible critique one can construct of the very best the other has to offer" (Altman & Davies, 2003, p. 149). It is difficult to see how Altman and Davies are following this commitment in their own response to Richards. Altman and Davies go on to critique the ways in which two other articles recently appearing in the *Journal of the American Psychoanalytic Association* (a publication singled out because Richards was serving at the time on its editorial board) reflect their notion of what they derisively term "pseudodialogue." It might be noted that the very gesture of labeling something in this way seems inherently opposed to the notion of constructive dialogue the authors recommend.

Echoing a common theme, Altman and Davies propose that the most distinctive quality of relational thinking is "diversity" – thus, the field's defining feature is in a sense proposed to be its very resistance to definition. This is reminiscent of Ghent's (1992) statement that there is no such thing as a relational analyst, and Spezzano's (1998) notion that relational analysts might almost be understood as a community of individuals without anything in common. Such claims serve a significant function in protecting relational thinking from criticism; in this light, any generalized objection to the relational movement can potentially be dismissed simply on face value. Altman and Davies also shift into contesting who holds the "middle ground" in psychoanalytic theorizing. When debate comes to rest upon this notion, the intent to explore a dialectical tension appears to have been abandoned in favor of pursuing a discourse that is frankly political. This is perhaps one of the inherent dangers in actively promoting a theoretical dialectics – that discourse devolves into claims about who is being most reasonably open-minded. Nevertheless, what the exchange between Richards on the one hand and Altman and Davies on the other perhaps expresses, in form if not necessarily in content, is precisely what the field has for so long lacked – a willingness to engage despite fundamental differences. What seems most signifiant and perhaps even encouraging about a conversation of this kind is simply the fact of its taking place in the first place, warts and all, so that the respective pleas for humility and constructive dialogue in a sense succeed despite themselves.

In contrast to a heated debate of this kind, contemporary object relations theorist Frank Summers (2008) is suspicious of the ways in which theoretical pluralism might not always move beyond facile accommodations. Calling for an engagement between psychoanalytic schools that extends beyond mere tolerance to reflect a challenging of core assumptions, Summers perceives the emergence of genuine dialogue as an unfolding from sectarian warfare, through polite tolerance, to a true willingness to listen. This outlook seems laudable, yet it might be restrictive to assume that genuine engagement emerges only out of polite tolerance. Reflecting Summers' phenomenological predisposition, this perspective perhaps under-estimates the extent to which the questioning of biases often implies deep (i.e., unconscious) conflict. Summers (2013b) suggests that the use of theory should not entail making presuppositions, but rather self-critically assuming a position or stance towards the world (p. 17). This ideal seems not to credit the extent to which the world is only made available to us for self-conscious reflection as a consequence of our pre-conscious/pre-reflective ideas about it. While the hope Summers expresses that the analyst should be self-aware in assuming a given clinical position can be said to reflect a basically sound intention, in emphasizing the claim that we should know where we are theoretically there seems to be a danger of coming to underestimate our own unconsciousness.

Relational thinking has been centrally concerned to emphasize the ways in which the analyst's subjectivity is constantly shaping the clinical situation. As Harris (2011) states: "Silence is no guarantee of opacity or even psychic space available for the analysand to work in" (p. 718). This observation clearly has implications for what we might expect in regards to negotiating theoretical divergence. Jessica Benjamin (1990) stresses that breakdown in communication should not be considered indicative of a relational failure: "If the clash of two wills is an inherent part of intersubjective relations, then no perfect environment can take the sting from the encounter with otherness" (p. 44). In a similar sense, Aron (1996) encourages us to reflect that the relational attitude becomes cloying without sufficient recognition of autonomy. This same tendency can be discerned at the level of theory, when the intent to include opposing positions threatens to grow overbearing and thus fails to allow for fundamental difference.

Traditionally, critics of psychoanalysis have often drawn attention to the problems arising out of the idea of resistance, since any truth claim grounding itself in this concept appears to be unverifiable. Charles Taylor (1985) refers to this tendency as the "heads-I-win, tails-you-lose" predicament (p. 123). In a professed willingness to include opposing views within its own discourse, relational thinking is liable to achieve something quite similar in effectively seeking to make it impossible to take a stance that is legitimately opposed to the relational one. In attempting to reflect both sides of any given dispute, the relational outlook is in danger of portraying itself as though having somehow transcended its own theoretical commitments. Thus, in reflecting a tendency to enfold all difference within the overarching rubric of relational dialectics, we might see recapitulated at a theoretical level precisely one of the most fundamental criticisms leveled at relational thinking clinically – that, owing to a reticence to evoke opposition, the other remains inadequately recognized.

While psychoanalysis obviously benefits from attempting to reengage its own disavowed parts, an excessive emphasis on open-mindedness succeeds only in rendering us less receptive to difference. Žižek (2001) has drawn attention to the fashion in which overbearing respect for the other can imply an inverted form of bigotry. In this light, an ostensible acceptance of difference might need to be moderated with a sense of irony, a tolerance for being significantly offended, and the adoption of a perspective that emphasizes engaged conflict rather than seeking to emphasize an underlying harmony. In practice, the intent to be more inclusive – particularly when expressed as a desire to reconcile differences – is often counter-productive. Nevertheless, from women's liberation through the civil rights movement to the legalization of gay marriage, this impulse has also proven inestimably valuable. Thus, in the context of psychoanalytic theorizing, considerable care must be taken so that the more constructive aspects of this intent be preserved without occluding the recognition of difference.

Relational commitments

If relational thinking is reflective both of a particular psychoanalytic school of thought and of an ethos of inclusion that extends beyond this, one of the aims of the present work is to explore how the latter might be undermined by some of the theoretical ideas conventionally associated with the former. What, then, are the more generalizable claims of relational thinking? Following Ghent (1989), in the present context those approaches considered relational are understood to "have in common the stress on the experiential and relational aspects of human development, of psychopathology, and of the therapeutic efforts at relieving psychopathology" (p. 177). In contrast to the classical paradigm, wherein relationships are conceived as being shaped and determined by drives, Greenberg and Mitchell (1983) point to a widespread reversal of this claim and express their belief that the drives are fundamentally constituted in relationships. Drawing on a wealth of psychoanalytic literature in support of this position, the reversal thus portrayed has exerted considerable influence.

Greenberg and Mitchell perceive a commonality between American interpersonal thinking and British object relations theory, as reflected in the emphasis on "actual" relationships in distinction to fantasied others – Sullivan's notion of detailed inquiry and Fairbairn's de-eroticizing of the libido both attempt to place a renewed emphasis on the causality of the social world. In placing this kind of stress on the social, however, concern has arisen that the relational trend in psychoanalysis emphasizes the causative nature of human relationships to such an extent that Freud's theoretical shift from focusing on the influence of an actual trauma to emphasizing the role of unconscious fantasy is in danger of being reversed. Grotstein (2000) argues for the enduring importance of a recognition of fantasy life as the basis for psychic change, and perceives that this recognition is endangered where the tropes of the imagination are conceived as a product of our relationships with others rather than being pre-given with our biology (p. 37). Similarly, Mills (2012) is concerned to show that when the drives are conceptualized in terms of our relationships with others, they are effectively conceived to have their origins in conscious experience (p. 9). With this in mind, Mills argues that the relational turn in psychoanalysis has seen the field lose much of its depth in coming to reflect a social psychology of consciousness. In response to claims of this nature, Aron (1996) points out that the term "relational" was itself adopted in an effort to distance the movement from the superficiality sometimes associated with the term "social" (p. 27). Relational theorists wish to accommodate theoretical positions with an intrapsychic basis as well as those more explicitly concerned with external relationships – Greenberg and Mitchell's original intention in seeking to combine object relational and interpersonal approaches is reflective precisely of the effort to try and overcome the clear split between these two positions. However, in so far as the intrapsychic dimension of relational thinking reflects a position that the inner world is *only* a product of our relationships with others, many will continue to feel that the charge of superficiality is not unjustified.

Freud's efforts to maintain a properly psychological outlook have often been met with incomprehension. The challenge to conventional assumptions that such an approach registers has perhaps contributed to the acceptance of relational discourse which, with its common-sense appeal to the social, de-emphasizes the foundational role of unconscious fantasy. A year after the publication of Greenberg and

Mitchell's trailblazing text, Masson (1984) spearheaded an influential attack on psychoanalysis (still dominated at that time by classical thinking) claiming that Freud's emphasis on fantasy life results in a neglect of the reality of childhood sexual abuse. While powerfully effective in its mobilization of emotion, clearly a reading of this kind does a disservice to Freud who never argued against the view that an actual instance of sexual abuse can be traumatically harmful. As Elliot (2013) observes, this argument implies that Freud's emphasis on fantasy can be considered reflective of a fundamentally escapist psychology, while in practice Freud considered fantasy to be the very medium through which the individual engages the world (p. 71).[2]

The extent to which a thoroughgoing psychological position challenges conventional thinking is indicated by a reflection of James Hillman's (1983): "Statements from any field [...] become psychological, or revelations of psyche when their literalism is subverted to allow their suppositions to appear. The strategy implies that psychology cannot be limited to being one field among others since psyche permeates all fields and things" (p. 27). Such an outlook radically questions the notion that psychoanalysis should be negotiating ground with the theoretical claims of other disciplines. From this perspective, Kohut (1959) seems well-justified in suggesting that we should avoid adopting the findings of social psychology or biology in support of psychoanalytic investigation, which he considers a fundamentally introspective method of inquiry. Hillman and Kohut's thinking is in sharp distinction to the recent psychoanalytic emphasis on interdisciplinary dialogue, since both figures point to the necessity of affirming the psychological paradigm with its commitment to subjective experience over and against the claims of other fields. While Ghent (1992) states that the relational position is fundamentally psychological, this statement might need to be measured with a recognition of the extent to which a genuinely psychological point of view challenges popular assumptions. Unfortunately, this fact continues to be obscured by virtue of the extent to which academic psychology draws from the fields of sociology and biology in order to avoid the scientific embarrassment inevitably registered in a genuine commitment to subjectivity.

One of the most notable ways in which Greenberg and Mitchell (1983) succeed in reflecting this commitment is expressed in their significant claim that the distinction between drive and relationship suggests a philosophical difference that is ultimately a question of personal preference. Wachtel (2007) argues that this was an unfortunate betrayal of empiricism (pp. 85–86), yet in so doing fails to acknowledge that the commitment to empiricism he professes is the expression of his own philosophical bias. He goes on to firmly state: "Human beings are physical beings, biological organisms. No viable theory can ignore this reality, and even to minimize it is to reduce one's thinking to vapid evasions" (p. 90). Again, this is an untrammeled confession of faith, the truth content of which Wachtel apparently takes to be so self-evident that it remains unjustified. It is one thing to observe that human beings can usefully be considered biological organisms, but it is quite another to insists that psychology must bow to this fact. Classical theorist Morris Eagle (2007) offers another strong example of the totalizing claims that tend to creep in around scientific discourse. Eagle argues that the pluralism of psychoanalytic schools is not in the best interests of the profession's future, and that this tendency needs to be counteracted with recourse to the findings of empirical science. In ostensibly arguing against psychoanalytic insularity, Eagle urges that the profession should reach out to integrate the findings of other disciplines. That the disciplines Eagle endorses reaching out to clearly reflect his own theoretical biases goes unaddressed.

The populist and thoroughly reasonable nature of these arguments from science is difficult to oppose. In the present intellectual climate, however, a powerful response is suggested in drawing attention to the extent that these claims are contingent upon the restrictive assumptions of a Western scientistic mindset. In the English-speaking clinical world, the theme of pragmatism imposingly expresses itself as a demand for the grounded reassurance of results. Given this frame of reference, divergences from the common view are readily framed as speculative and perhaps even unethical. Mitchell and Harris (2004) draw attention to the influence of William James on American psychoanalytic thinking, and endorse his suspicion of foundational truth. While a suspicion of this kind can serve in counteracting the absolutizing claims of science, the pragmatic reliance on measurable results only goes to support them. It therefore seems worth noting that a suspicion towards foundational truth in itself reflects a foundational commitment. The appeal to results can readily come to be imbued with a certain humanitarian self-righteousness, the nature of which does nothing to address the extent to which protecting *the average person's interests* might have more to do with maintaining established power structures. Leading relationalists like Mitchell (1993), Renik (2006), and Wachtel (2007) all endorse the notion that psychoanalysis should come to model itself on a form of development grounded in pragmatic rationality. Pragmatism, however, is hardly a panacea for all our theoretical ills. As Jacob Needleman (1975) tellingly states in respect to the limits of the pragmatic outlook: "When an idea or theory 'works' it always does so relative to what we are asking of reality. If we have narrow intentions, our discoveries – no matter how ingenious – can never be bigger than our basic intentions" (p. 14).

As though in response to limitations of this kind, the potentially more radical aspect of relational thinking has been expressed in an epistemological shift towards constructivism. Irwin Hoffman (1998) argues that in defining the nature of the relational position, the movement from drive to relationship is in fact secondary. He suggests that the more fundamental tendency defining the significance of relational thinking lies in the epistemological shift away from positivism (p. 135). Where classical analysis in America has traditionally grounded itself in the assumptions of medical science, relationalists, following the pluralistic sensibilities of postmodern philosophy, have sought to reflect the notion that all truth claims are context dependent. Social constructivist thinking draws attention to the ways in which our ideas are historically and culturally contingent. The constructivist focus is considered by Hoffman to offer a more effective basis from which to talk about the change in contemporary analytic thinking, since this standpoint may reflect a less direct reaction against the claims of a one-person psychology:

In our zeal to correct the overemphasis in classical psychoanalytic theory on the individual dimension, it is important that we not swing to an overemphasis on the relational dimension, thereby isolating each from the other. The shift to a social-constructivist paradigm for understanding the psychoanalytic situation certainly does not require such a reversal. If anything, it requires a synthesis of the two perspectives with appropriate redefinitions of each in the light of their interdependence.

(Hoffman, 1998, p. 162)

While the emphasis on relationship in distinction to drive has often been received within classical circles by means of a strategy of accommodation[3] (e.g., Dunn, 1995), the emergence of constructivist thinking has elicited considerably more direct opposition. Eagle (2003) appears to be reflecting the views of many classical analysts in arguing that the postmodern-relational emphasis on the context-dependence of truth results in untenable claims about the nature of reality and an unwarranted devaluation of the individual. Eagle's position expresses an underlying commitment to the enduring value of Western metaphysics, and a belief that psychoanalysis should ground itself in the physical sciences rather than lose its way in pursuing the false turn of postmodern thinking.

Whitehead (1926) defines metaphysics succinctly as that field of endeavor "which seeks to discover the general ideas which are indispensably relevant to the analysis of everything that happens" (p. 84). Under the influence of Nietzsche and Heidegger, postmodernism has rejected the notion that such knowledge can be secured and thus denies the metaphysical postulate of a unified human subject. Defenders of one-person thinking have contended that such claims are antithetical to establishing a basis from which psychoanalysis can justify itself as a clinical practice. Owing to the medical emphasis of the American classical tradition, however, objections of this kind have often been expressed with recourse to the perceived authority of science (e.g., Langs, 1993), rather than in more extensively examining the clinical problems that come to be raised with the notion that all knowledge is context dependent. Thus, in attempting to protect drive psychology from the constructivist trend in relational psychoanalysis, classical thinking has often relied upon a scientific discourse which itself tends to shirk recognition of its own metaphysical commitments.

Relativism has been refuted since the time of Plato with the observation that Protagoras' *man is the measure of all things* itself reflects an absolute truth claim. Maurice Blondel (1893/1984) gives further voice to this problem when he states: "One cannot exclude metaphysics except by a metaphysical critique" (p. 358). In distinction to the kind of relativism associated with much postmodern thinking, Mills (2005) wishes to argue that psychoanalysis is unavoidably a metaphysical undertaking. He writes: "The instant we open our eyes and orient our senses to what we apprehend before us, we have already made metaphysical commitments – reality is presupposed" (p. 280). Advancing this point further, we might even argue that our eyes are opened precisely in making these commitments. Owing to the phenomenological and postmodern leanings of relational psychoanalysis, however, theoretical arguments of this kind have a good deal less rhetorical leverage than the problems arising from the apparent threat of relativism.

Orange (1992) objects to what she perceives signified in "constructivism." She takes exception to adopting this term as a basis for psychoanalytic inquiry on the grounds that it fails to "provide any positive account of what constitutes scientific progress or psychoanalytic cure" (p. 562). In her view, constructivism is untenable as a psychoanalytic epistemology since it cannot accommodate the notion of development. The "perspectival realism" Orange proposes as an alternative endorses the notion that we each have a contextually dependent view of an objectively existent reality, the ultimate nature of which can never be fully grasped. This question of ungraspability, however, is not posited to the exclusion of progress or the viability of at least gaining a more accurate perception of truth over time – she uses the example of the countless photographs taken of the Brooklyn Bridge, each of which captures only something of the bridge itself in its factual existence independent of perception. Orange states that the approach she espouses is significant in that it avoids delegitimizing the analysand's experience as a "mere construct," and instead recognizes experience as being "of something." This claim might be considered somewhat questionable, since it seems the notion that the analysand's experience is only reflective of a context-dependent view of a much greater whole is liable to have a similarly invalidating effect. This is reflected in an article by Ringstrom (2010) who, in the course of endorsing Orange's approach, repeatedly refers to the role of our "optical delusions." With this possibly unfortunate wording in mind, it seems all the more noteworthy that Ringstrom perceives the epistemology of perspectival realism to be generally representative not only of the underlying position of Orange's intersubjectivist[4] colleagues, but also of the wider relational movement (p. 198). As is evident from Hoffman's (1992) earlier response to Orange, their debate is indeed largely terminological and the two theorists appear to be arguing for much the same position. Aron (1996) also subscribes to a similar view. Like Orange, he prefers the term "perspectivism" to "constructivism," doing so explicitly out of a concern that the latter might be misconstrued as too radical.

Such reticence to openly speak of "constructivism" neglects the wide range of positions that this term conventionally encompasses. The word is in fact used a great deal more broadly than Orange portrays, and can certainly be considered inclusive of her own position. Though Aron's political decision to avoid this term is understandable, such a move has the effect of foreclosing some of the potentially more challenging aspects of relationality by distancing the weaker forms of constructivism typically associated with relational thinking from the stronger and more radical forms. Weak-form outlooks are typified by the approach of John Searle (1998), who distinguishes between "brute facts" and "institutional facts" – the former he regards as fundamental and irreducible, while the latter arise out of social convention. This position is reflected in Orange's Brooklyn Bridge metaphor, where photographs of the bridge reflect context-dependent renderings of the brute fact of the bridge itself. Orange (2003) explicitly describes her perspectival realism as "an important middle road between positivism and radical constructivism" (p. 81). Strong-form constructivism, by contrast, refuses the distinction between brute facts and institutional facts, and maintains that all truth claims are context dependent. The weaker form of constructivism usually favored by relationalists is seemingly adopted to protect psychoanalytic discourse from collapsing into a relativism that would offer no basis upon which to found psychoanalytic truth claims. Thus, the constructivist line of relational thinking often dubbed "perspectivism" or "per-spectivalism" has sought to accommodate itself to a common-sense view of the world that can be reconciled with contemporary science, and which also evades the potential danger of falling into a technically unsupportable relativism. It is impor-tant to recognize, however, that while such an approach seems at first glance quite reasonable and perhaps even open-minded, it can also exhibit an aggressive and domineering undertow – endorsing a view of this kind enables the preservation of certain aspects of an underlying worldview from strong-form constructivist criticism while, in deference to pluralism/postmodernity, simultaneously embracing an appealing veneer of weak-form constructivist rhetoric. This approach expresses a potent ideological mix demonstrating the extent to which, despite significant efforts to question many of the essentialisms associated with the American classical tradition, contemporary psychoanalysis continues to assert the theoretical primacy of the reality principle. The problem this position inevitably poses is in explaining how a line is to be drawn between the domain of facts on the one hand, and social constructions on the other – relying on pragmatic common sense is hardly an acceptable strategy, since it is precisely the viability of common sense that con-structivist thinking potentially throws into doubt. If we insist upon preserving the unquestioned factual status of that which strikes us to be most incontrovertibly true, then rather than reflecting an ethos of pluralism constructivism is liable to serve only as a means to undermine any position that doesn't happen to match our own.[5]

A restrictiveness of this kind might not seem necessary, however, if it were to be recognized that stronger forms of constructivism needn't imply the complete denial of objectivity. For example, while an extreme postmodernist like Donna Haraway (1990) goes so far as to posit the immune system as "an elaborate icon for principal systems of symbolic and material 'difference' in late capitalism" (p. 204), thus extending de Beauvoir's maxim that one is not born a woman to suggest that one is not even born an organism, she is willing to accept that bodies have a special status as a "material semiotic actor" (p. 208). Although Haraway suggests that the idea of nature is no longer sustainable and with it "the transcendent authorization of interpretation" (p. 153), she nevertheless accepts that "the world for us may be thoroughly denatured, but it is not any less consequential" (p. 209). This is a subtle claim that perhaps points beyond the confines of conventional postmodern thinking. The difficulty many have with such a statement is partly consequent upon the extent to which constructivist thought has tended to restrict itself to epistemological critique so as to negate conventional truth claims, rather than in building new ways of thinking about how the binding nature of reality might thus be conceptualized. Haraway appears to suggest that the subjectively constituted nature of our truth claims does not prevent these claims from becoming in some contingent sense objectively valid. Perhaps the most convincing recent psychoanalytic expression of this idea has been offered by Donnel Stern (1997) in his approach to the given and the made: "we are referring not to the contrast between humanly constructed meaning and what came before it, but to what we find preconstructed and what we make of it" (p. 6).

In further teasing apart different approaches to constructivism, Kukla (2000) distinguishes between "constitutive" constructivists and "causal" constructivists – the former he defines as expressing a belief that our knowledge claims are merely reflective of human activity, while the latter suggest that human belief actively sustains the objective facticity of the world around us. Kukla observes that most strong-form constructivists generally maintain a constitutive position, yet they often slip into speaking in such a way as to imply a more causal position (p. 22). This tendency is perhaps reflected in Haraway's referring to the consequentiality of the world despite its status as a construct. Kukla offers his own example by citing the following passage from Latour and Woolgar (1986, p. 180):

> We do not wish to say that facts do not exist nor that there is no such thing as reality. In this simple sense our position is not relativist. Our point is that "out-there-ness" is the *consequence* of scientific work rather than its *cause*.

Causal constructivism appears to offer a radical position that nevertheless finds room for something approaching objective fact, yet in registering the truth of the world as shifting and still in some sense arbitrary, this outlook continues to lack a transcendent basis upon which to ground action – a need which appears unavoidable for the clinical application of psychoanalysis. While weak-form constructivism endorses the notion of a stable universe that is assumed to effectively anchor interpretation, causal constructivism appears to suggest that the laws to which we are bound are arbitrary and in some degree manipulable. Although clinicians might draw conclusions from this position that are equivalent to those belonging to weak-form constructivism (i.e., that we can justifiably ground our interpretations in reality as presently understood) the subjective factor now explicitly implicated in sustaining the objective situation must inevitably draw us to engage metaphysics in search of an account not just of how human action *has* been grounded, but of how it *should* be grounded. Thus, if the more radical constructivist position is to be endorsed as a basis for contemporary psychoanalytic thinking, we are drawn into metaphysical challenges that the weak form seemingly evades. As will be shown (Chapter 1), however, this is misleading, for the only reason weak-form constructivism seems to offer a means of anchoring psychoanalytic interpretation without explicitly engaging metaphysics is as a consequence of the extent to which this paradigm continues to rely on the underlying assumptions of empirical science.

Outlining an approach

How might contemporary psychoanalytic practice develop a more rigorously pluralistic outlook without submitting to relativism? I contend that the relational ethos can only avoid falling back on the underlying assumptions of Western science by adopting a philosophical framework that more directly addresses the role of founding principles. Metaphysics repressed returns as fundamentalism – whether religious or secular. Relational thinking therefore requires a way of thinking the metaphysical in clinical practice so as to be consistent with the relational outlook's own foundational commitment to diversity. I suggest that depth psychology already has the theoretical resources to approach meeting this need, yet remains shy of doing so owing to the field's continuing struggle to properly accept its own theoretical terms. Consistent with this claim, the present work is informed by a perspective with its roots in the classical German philosophy out of which psychodynamic thinking was itself born – a perspective which is therefore inherently compatible with psychoanalytic work. Transpersonal theorist and historian of ideas Richard Tarnas (1991) portrays this outlook as expressing an emerging shift in the history of Western ideas that he terms "participatory." Tarnas suggests that the participatory worldview was initiated by Goethe, and can be traced through the work of such figures as Schiller, Schelling, Hegel, Coleridge, Emerson, and Rudolf Steiner. Perspectives associated with this imputed shift express in various ways the idea that the changing nature of mind is reflected in the shifting nature of objective reality. This outlook challenges the neo-Kantian tendency to perceive subjectivity as a distortion of truth, and argues instead that subjective mediation is the basis upon which individuals participate co-creatively in the self-disclosure of the world. Tarnas writes:

> The new conception fully acknowledged the validity of Kant's critical insight, that all human knowledge of the world is in some sense determined by subjective principles; but instead of considering these principles as belonging ultimately to the separate human subject, and therefore not grounded in the world inde-pendent of human cognition, this participatory conception held that these subjective principles are in fact an expression of the world's own being, and that the human mind is ultimately the organ of the world's own process of self-revelation. In this view, the essential reality of nature is not separate, self-contained, and complete in itself, so that the human mind can examine it "objectively" and register it from without. Rather, nature's unfolding truth emerges only with the active participation of the human mind. Nature's reality is not merely phenomenal, nor is it independent and objective; rather, it is something that comes into being through the very act of human cognition. Nature becomes intelligible to itself through the human mind.
>
> (Tarnas, 1991, pp. 433–434)

A position of this kind offers an interesting response to Thomas Nagel's (1986) observation that in recent times the notion of objectivity is both overvalued and underestimated (p. 5). While positivism privileges the objective frame of reference to such an extreme that it would sometimes seek to deny the existence of subjectivity altogether, within the Continental tradition historicist and poststructural strands of thinking disavow the objective standpoint to an extent that can seem equally untenable. The participatory perspective proposes that our experience should not be considered reflective of a reified positivist conception of truth, but nor should it be treated as merely phenomenal. Instead, objective nature is thought to be actualized through subjective cognition. Heron (1996) has termed the kind of ontology that emerges from a participatory outlook subjective-objective: "It is subjective because it is only known through the form the mind gives it; and it is objective because the mind interpenetrates the given cosmos which it shapes" (p. 11). Participatory thinking clearly bears a significant relationship with causal constructivism. In distinction to a constructivist position, however, participatory thinking remains explicitly committed to a metaphysics of the subject. In this light, a participatory outlook seeks to radically reimagine the relationship between subject and object, thus reflecting something of the traditional belief in a correspondence between microcosm and macrocosm as expressed in such disparate traditions as Christianity, Buddhism, Vedanta, Taoism, Platonism, Kabbalah, and Hermeticism. Broadening the notion of relationality to embrace our relationship with the cosmos, Tarnas contends this movement in thought has a fundamentally moral connotation:

> At the heart of this epistemological shift, I believe, is a moral shift; namely, that to have appropriated all intelligence in the universe as only ours is an act of a moral nature and has moral consequences. We essentially moved from an interdependent relationship with the universe to an independent relationship to the universe, with deeply problematic consequences.
>
> (Tarnas, et al., 2001, p. 43)

While challenges to Cartesianism have become a mainstay of contemporary psychoanalytic theorizing, the present work argues that it is often in mounting these challenges that the field's underlying commitment to materialism shows itself most clearly by privileging the objective fact of the body over the fantasy of the subject. In a participatory frame of reference, by contrast, rather than conceptually dissolving the subject into the object, the subjective is effectively posited as an active principle animating the domain of objectivity. Tarnas (1991) demonstrates how such a worldview might offer a response to problems raised in the philosophy of science. He cites Karl Popper's Kantian contention that because the human mind has no access to a priori truth, scientific myth making only garners practical results as a consequence of what amounts to a fortunate overlap with the objective world. Perceiving this explanation to be unsatisfactory, Tarnas reasons that a participatory perspective offers a more satisfying explanation in positing that the human mind's myth-making capacity, when it apparently succeeds in this fashion, reflects a participatory resonance with the evolving nature of the cosmos. From this perspective, the question that Kuhn and Feyerabend's work raises as to why one scientific paradigm wins out over another can now be understood in terms of a more fundamental sense of what rings most true. In this frame of reference science cannot rightly be considered as nothing but another myth, but neither can myth be portrayed as "merely" subjective.

Significantly, the participatory turn is not offered by Tarnas as a formalized philosophical framework, but rather as a means of talking about a recurring theme in the history of ideas that has been insufficiently recognized within mainstream academia. Sherman (2008) suggests that the emergence of participatory thinking in the West can be traced as far back as Ancient Greece, and can be roughly divided into three historical phases: the formal (associated with Plato), the existential (associated with Aquinas), and the creative (a phase still developing, and which largely correlates with the paradigm identified by Tarnas). Formal participation arises with Plato out of the growing need to maintain relations between the human and the divine. Plato adopts the term *methexis* to denote the constitutive fashion in which humans are conceived to participate in the nature of the eternal Forms. Thus the Platonic Forms are posited in distinction from a natural world in which they are at the same time immediately implicated. While this approach offers a way of understanding *what* a being is, Sherman suggests that it remained for the existential participation of Aquinas to offer a means of thinking *why* a being is. Aquinas's accent on the primordial act of being gives rise to a participatory vision wherein the Absolute calls to the subject and elicits a response – participation in this light is inclusive of the question of Platonic essence, but also goes further to embrace the notion of existence as an ongoing act of creation gifted by God. In both formal and existential participation, however, creativity is attributed solely to the Absolute. Only with the more recent idea of creative participation is a place found for the agency of the individual. Sherman points to the particular importance of Schelling in voicing this outlook – a figure who, it should be noted, is also widely credited as having established the philosophical notion of the unconscious.

The radical emphasis that a contemporary approach to participation places on the creative nature of the subject offers a significant opportunity from which to develop a more pluralistically nuanced approach to psychoanalytic practice. While there is a broad willingness to acknowledge that relational thinking does indeed reflect certain locally determined theoretical commitments (Mitchell & Harris, 2004), it is debatable how far this recognition has translated into a discourse that would seek to address this as a potential limit in working with patients – theoretical differences are typically understood to exist between analysts, rather than being more significantly expressed as an issue arising between analyst and analysand. In treatment, the notion of subjectivity is in effect considered as a variable that can be approached *within* the context of a theoretical framework. Even if the analyst's theory is admitted to be an expression of his or her own subjectivity, that which is understood by the notion of subjectivity is itself inevitably an expression of the very theory from which the clinician seeks to gain reflective distance – that is, recognizing the role of subjectivity can only occur within the framework of our own subjectively determined conceptions.

If the clinician is to more effectively address the role of their own predisposition in dictating to the clinical interaction, it will not suffice merely to recognize one's position as being reflective of a particular context since the clinician's understanding of context is itself indicative of the problem. Rather than seek to relativize subjects in relationship to an implied question of objectivity, a more coherent response could lie in theoretically empowering subjectivity itself. A move of this kind can be expected by definition to promote a greater respect for the patient while simultaneously recognizing the ubiquity of the analyst's own power and the clash of wills thus implied. In adopting such an outlook, the ethical needs of clinical work might be better addressed in emphasizing a philosophical approach that would seek to explore founding principles in fallibilistic orientation to the other.

Working towards such a position, the present text seeks to offer an initial impression of the ways in which participatory thinking might suggest a powerful basis from which to reconfigure debates within contemporary psychoanalysis. Aron and Starr (2012) express their hope that a new effort will emerge to integrate drive and relational thinking that will be reflective of the dialectical ethos foregrounded in contemporary discourse (p. 37). The approach offered here reflects an initial attempt to meet this challenge and, in doing so, to establish the initial contours of a "post-relational" discourse. This designation is intended to indicate an approach which, in its reengagement with the metaphysical, registers a significant challenge to relational thinking – in its spirit, however, the underlying intent is posited to remain true to the relational ideal of pluralism, if not always to the original assumptions of relational theorizing. While the movement inaugurated by Greenberg and Mitchell (1983) figures an endeavor to integrate interpersonal, neo-Freudian and object relational schools, the post-relational is here conceptualized as a second integrative moment that would seek to reconnect with those figures and ideas from the field's history that have not yet been adequately resuscitated in mainstream conversation – in particular, I am concerned to explore how elements of post-Jungian and transpersonal thinking might supplement the work of fringe figures like Bion and Lacan to stimulate and challenge mainstream conversation. This perspective is also in keeping with Aron and Atlas's (2015) sense that relational thinking needs to engage more substantially with the Jungian lineage, and Tennes's (2007) call for a new paradigm shift in mainstream thinking that will more effectively address the question of spirituality. Finding support in the recent outpouring of excellent scholarly work that would seek to locate psychoanalytic practice in the history of ideas (Taylor, 1999, 2009; Shamdasani, 2004, 2012; Žižek, 2007; Makari, 2008; Ffytche, 2011; McGrath, 2012; Nicholls & Liebscher, 2012; Mills, 2014), this endeavor reflects an ongoing effort to restore psychoanalytic thinking to its proper intellectual context, and to challenge the still widespread notion that psychoanalysis is "the creation of one man" (Greenberg & Mitchell, 1983, p. 21). The extent to which Freud has been portrayed as the field's founding father has had a restrictive impact on the fashion in which the psychodynamic profession interprets itself, minimizing the contributions of Freud's contemporaries and isolating the profession from the intellectual context out of which it emerged.[6] Relationalists have done a great deal to recognize figures from the field's past that were marginalized by the classical mainstream, yet this project has been somewhat limited having been motivated largely out of the particular biases associated with the relational approach.

By invoking the intellectual context out of which psychodynamic psychology emerged, the most deep-seated and essential commitments of the field might be addressed more directly. This undertaking is guided not merely with the intent of challenging latent assumptions, but in seeking to more rigorously establish the ground upon which psychoanalytic practice ultimately stands. In contemporary thinking, the tendency to emphasize experiential data over theoretical presupposition can lead to our losing sight of the extent to which psychoanalytic interaction is unavoidably founded in theoretical commitments (Greenberg, 1994; Aron, 1996; Spezzano, 1996b; Pine, 1998). These commitments are, in a significant sense, prior to any question of a divergence between approaches, since they find expression in the very situation out of which the notion of clinical data can emerge in the first place – that is, the commonality most readily discerned between all schools of psychodynamic thinking is established most basically in the clinical situation itself.

In the first chapter of the present work, this locus of psychoanalytic commonality is unfolded by exploring the notion of clinical intent. Implicit in this exploration is a recognition that certain foundational assumptions have already been made by the clinician in assuming their role as such. Among these assumptions we might speculatively include a belief in the value of the individual, a belief in the value of intimacy, a belief in the value of privacy, and a belief that there is a meaning to analytic work which is ethically consistent with the needs and assumptions that bring individuals to treatment. In pursuing these themes I consider the clinical assumptions of mainstream psychoanalytic practice at the present time, and examine the underlying claims being made about human nature and the notion of mental illness. I argue that the viability of psychoanalytic practice is threatened not only as a consequence of social pressures exerted from outside the field, but also in the extent to which the theoretical underpinnings of contemporary thinking have come to question the value of such fundamental psychoanalytic ideas as the human subject and the unconscious. To actively build upon its deep significance as a cultural movement, I suggest that psychoanalytic practice needs to deemphasize the notion of cure in favor of focusing more directly on the promotion of a postmodern ethics of difference.

Having argued for the importance to be construed in the notion of the subject, I proceed to explore the status of this idea in the field at present. Drawing attention to the ideological dangers associated with systems thinking, Chapter 2 shows how relational theorizing may fail to sufficiently recognize the value of the individual and of introspection. Given the conceptual need that a contemporary clinical approach direct itself towards recognition of the analysand as a creative agent of change, I show that despite recent interest both in critiquing Cartesianism and in arguing for pluralistic conceptions of selfhood, the notion of a partially self-determined and distinct subject continues to play an essential role in psychodynamic thinking.

However, in light of recent efforts to respond to the challenges of postmodernity, the importance of this idea has come to be rhetorically minimized. While this tendency has been valuable in giving rise to new ways of thinking about therapeutic interaction, it remains theoretically essential that these challenges be contextualized in such a way as to recognize the primary value of the individual. In responding to this perceived need, I seek to establish a position that might offer an approach to contemporary philosophy befitting the nature of clinical practice. With particular emphasis on the work of philosopher Dieter Henrich, it is argued that restoring the notion of the subject requires an ethically motivated return to metaphysics.

Given the role that metaphysical presupposition inevitably plays in shaping our interactions with others, it remains to be asked how contemporary psychoanalysis might engage more directly with the challenges thus implied. The need of doing so becomes most apparent when considering the question of spirituality. Addressing the seeming decline of drive theory, I explore recent approaches to motivation and draw attention to the need of making the problems associated with this theme more explicit. Chapter 3 thus seeks to question the limits of relational theory as a pluralistic discourse and shows how a cautious return to the notion of first principles might better serve recognition of the analysand as other. In pursuing this goal, I seek to place relational thinking in dialogue with a participatory reading of Jung's notion of the collective unconscious resulting in what is proposed to be a more effective basis from which to honor alterity in the analytic relationship. Emphasizing the creative role of conflict, an approach to archetypal thinking is outlined that might suggest a means of reconciling structural and poststructural tendencies within the field.

Finally, by way of amplification in respect to the relationship between self and world, in closing I consider how psychoanalysis conceives its role vis-à-vis present-day social issues, and explore what a psychoanalytic approach to collective change might look like from a participatory perspective. Clinical practice thus comes to be interpreted as an endeavor fundamentally concerned with bringing about a shift in the collective through recognition of the irreducible particularity of persons. If depth psychology is to remain true to a subjective ontology, reflecting this ideal at a political level entails challenging the conditions of what currently seems conceivable rather than in attempting to pragmatically accommodate to the perceived needs of the collective. It is argued that an outlook seeking to expressly meet present demands not only threatens to undermine the clinical efficacy of the profession, but reflects a fundamental disservice to the core values of the field. In keeping with the position outlined with respect to the question of cure, it is suggested that the fundamentally radical nature of psychoanalytic practice lies in facilitating the conditions for change rather than in seeking to enforce a particular notion of the way things should be.

1

CLINICAL INTENT

Over the course of the Middle Ages, "mental illness" had come to be understood largely in terms of divine or demonic intervention. By the 1600s, however, this conceptualization began to change. The decline of scholasticism saw human nature no longer interpreted in terms of supernatural causes, so much as defined by that which occurs most typically. In the early seventeenth century, Zacchias introduced the analysis of psychological symptoms, syndromes, and diseases (Cranefield & Federn, 1970). It was also during this period that the notion of "culture" arose, thus expressing a different (though not unrelated) kind of concern for the refinement of the individual. An increasing emphasis was coming to be placed on the idea of "nurture", such that a person's innate predisposition could more readily be considered distinct from the consequences of their life experience. Where a line had previously been drawn between the regular course of events and supernatural intercession, a new space had been created for the role of human action.

Changing ideas about mental illness naturally reflect the politics of the time. According to Ellenberger (1958), the "psychological" perspective is understood to have arisen in the eighteenth century, at which juncture the functions of the mind were divided into intellection, affectivity, and will. The particular significance placed on the notion of will seems intimately bound to the emerging idea of progress. Karl Jaspers (1931/1957) argues that while humanity has always exhibited a critical attitude toward its own circumstances, this tendency becomes significantly more apparent with the newfound emphasis on progress – for Jaspers, this is made most explicit in the events of the French Revolution. Meanwhile, the climate of upheaval was itself made subject to new forms of criticism. Jaspers nominates Kierkegaard as the first individual to undertake a "comprehensive critique of his time" (p. 10).

The call for a politics free from superstition necessarily required that a similar attitude be fostered towards people. Thus the newly emerging discipline of psychology was charged with exorcising the rich assemblage of angels and demons still exhibiting an influence over popular perception – a cast of characters which organized religion had sought to either integrate or else turn a blind eye to. Thus, if the foundation of the psychological perspective was significantly shaped by the desire to privilege reason, it was arguably at the cost of a more imaginatively vital connection to life. Schiller would introduce the notion of "disenchantment" (*Entzauberung*), a term later adopted by Max Weber in characterizing the desacralized condition of modernity. Over the course of the nineteenth century, a tension continued to develop between the perceived advances of civilization and an increasing sense of alienation in individuals. Regarding the relationship between these two tendencies, the year 1883 might be considered emblematic – with the publication of Emil Kraeplin's *Compendium der Psychiatrie*, and the first parts of Friedrich Nietzsche's *Thus Spake Zarathustra*, two lines of critical discourse were powerfully expressed that continue to play a fundamental role in shaping perceptions of the world around us.

Kraeplin's work is regarded as foundational for the emergence of modern psychiatry, and his commitment to the organic basis of mental illness continues to be reflected in contemporary approaches to diagnosis. He sought to organize psychopathology around cause, course, and prognosis. Since a clearly identifiable cause was rarely apparent, however, emphasis tended to be placed on the latter two domains (Makari, 2008, p. 207). This significant limitation continues to be expressed in the contemporary classification of mental disturbance, where a diagnosis based on prognosis inevitably entails dictating to the course of a presumed illness. Perhaps the most obvious example of this is given in the widely endorsed belief that a diagnosis of schizophrenia signifies the existence of an incurable disease – it may be more than coincidental that this diagnosis is now made with reference to a "psychosis spectrum" construed only on the basis of symptom duration and prognosis. The extent to which this classificatory approach defies invalidation is reflected where any outcome that contravenes expectation requires that the prior diagnosis be regarded as faulty, rather than question the fundamental assumptions of the system (Lotterman, 2015, pp. 7–8).[1]

In contrast to Kraeplin's concern for defining mental illness in persons, Nietzsche considered himself a physician of culture. This notion denotes a highly critical approach to society that was foreshadowed in the earlier work of Kierkegaard, and would find increasing expression in the climate of *fin de siècle* Europe. Max Nordau wrote an influential book published in 1892 entitled *Degeneration*, in which he argued that the spirit of the times was sick. Ironically, he saw Nietzsche as a prime example of the diseased heredity that he considered responsible for the wider ills of society. In this climate, the notion of cultural redemption also came to play a significant role in the reception of psychoanalytic ideas – the appearance of Freud's *Three Essays* made him extremely popular in the Viennese coffee houses, causing him to be embraced by those who believed that the deterioration of Habsburg Vienna was the consequence of excessive rules rather than biological degeneration.

Nietzsche's attitude towards sickness is complex, and naturally exerts a particular fascination by virtue of his own descent into madness. Nietzsche (1888/1992) writes: "Sickness itself can be a stimulant to life: only one has to be healthy enough for this stimulant" (p. 621). For Nietzsche, the sense of a certain kind of mundane well-being manifesting in an unseemly concern for one's own bodily functioning is perceived as a morbidity, the nature of which he defines as the refusal to become sick. Illness is the prerequisite to real health; a health that would incorporate illness. Thus nihilism is a necessary infirmity which the decadence of society resists. The collective is not threatened with sickness itself, so much as with the inability to fall sick in the first place. Nietzsche asks: "Is madness perhaps not necessarily the symptom of degeneration, decline, and the final stage of culture? Are there perhaps – a question for psychiatrists – neuroses of health?" (Nietzsche, 1886/1992, p. 21).

While Nietzsche's struggle with madness culminated in his being consumed by it, his critical approach to everyday perceptions of mental illness remains influential. French philosopher Edgar Morin (2008) makes a distinction between two kinds of madness: that of absolute incoherence, and that of absolute coherence. If Nietzsche could be said to have succumbed to the former, then the Kraeplinian system of diagnosis which has returned to ascendancy in contemporary clinical practice, might reasonably be thought indicative of the latter. In a related sense, historian of philosophy Pierre Hadot (2008) defines two approaches to nature: the Orphic, which is marked by philosophical or aesthetic modalities that adopt rational discourse or art; and the more forceful Promethean attitude which wrests life's secrets by means of mechanics, magic, or experimental method (p. 317). In the recent intellectual history of the West, it is the Promethean attitude that has come to hold sway almost exclusively. Since the Enlightenment, the notion of divine secrets came gradually to be re-framed as nature's secrets, with nature portrayed as a goddess jealously protecting this knowledge. Nature is raised up and understood in terms of higher powers, before being brought back down to Earth and conceived in terms of the task of an unmasking. It remains open to question whether this movement should be understood as occurring only once in the course of history as Hadot appears to assume, or if the tendency thus implied might be considered in some degree cyclical.

In fetishizing that to which it is attributed, the idea of nature is itself distinctly unnatural. Hadot (2008) suggests that the Greek notion of *physis* (usually translated as "nature") undergoes a shift in the fifth century BCE: no longer is the term used simply to refer to the manifest form of a thing, but rather to an inferred process by means of which a thing comes into being. This ultimately leads to a sense of "divinized nature" which emerges with Pliny the Elder so that *physis*, "which primitively signified an event, a process, or the realization of a thing, has come to mean the invisible power that realizes this event" (Hadot, 2008, p. 26). Nature, which had previously been considered in relative terms, is now conceptualized as that which conforms with the divine order. Leo Strauss (1989) goes so far as to suggest that the emergence of the concept of nature heralds the beginning of philosophy itself. Precisely as nature comes into existence *qua* idea, the existence of nature per se appears threatened. As with "the unconscious," the natural world seemingly withdraws in our efforts to approach it directly.

By introducing the notion of a final cause, Aristotle's teleology reflects a metaphysical endeavor to move beyond nature in order to explain it. In this scheme, nature is thought to have aims – a notion that has largely been excluded from psychoanalytic discourse since Adler and Jung's expulsion from the fold. Even with the more recent shift towards hermeneutics, psychoanalysis in the English-speaking world has tended to remain true to the Baconian empirical method that would seek to uncover the "laws of nature" without recourse to metaphysical postulates. It can therefore not be emphasized sufficiently that the extent to which the scientific method might claim to have transcended metaphysics is hugely contestable (Koyré, 1968; Kuhn, 1970; Lakatos, 1970). In so far as the term "nature" has come to be associated with the phenomena of the physical world, Timothy Morton (2007) describes this notion as "a transcendental term in a material mask" (p. 14). He also points out that traditional cultures tend to portray nature as a shape-shifter, and not as a fixed standard (p. 21). Are clinicians therefore to relinquish the idea of nature altogether and with it the basis for a coherent clinical stance, or might there be some question of incorporating this conception of nature as a shape-shifter into the clinical sensibility?

It is difficult to conceive what the outright denial of nature might amount to. In so far as the idea continues to influence us, it might be said to constitute what Jung (1921) terms a "psychological fact" (p. 42) – that is, the idea's ubiquity can be considered sufficient justification for its being taken seriously as a factor in human psychology. We might convince ourselves that the idea in question is counterproductive, but this doesn't annul it. In fact, the thought of nature seemingly imposes itself in some degree whenever we consciously determine a given course of action. Perhaps efforts to argue that mental illness does not in fact exist should be considered alongside similar arguments with respect to the question of race. While the notion that race exists as an objective fact can be shown to be false, it clearly remains a truth of our lived experience. In so long as this notion continues to significantly inform how we imagine the world around us, it continues to be meaningful. Thus claims to the effect that "race does not exist" would appear not only debatable, but possibly even offensive. Nagel (1986) argues that the contingency of a given language does nothing to diminish its normative reality for those inhabiting it (p. 11). In a similar vein, R.D. Laing (1967) writes: "There is no such 'condition' as 'schizophrenia,' but the label is a social fact and the social fact a *political event*" (p. 121, italics in original). A position of this sort does not require a denial of physical correlates to mental illness – there are also physical correlates to being labeled "black," even if the notion of "blackness" can be considered a construct.

As with reactions to the subject of race, in respect to mental illness the role played by suffering is central. These designations are indelibly associated with experiences of inequality and struggle. As such, they appear to demand a response. Nevertheless, recalling Nietzsche, we might question whether the apparently simple wish to avert another's perceived suffering is always in their best interests. Such a position is all too readily dismissed by the clinical mainstream as impractically speculative or perhaps even unethical, yet clearly a response of this kind can in no way be considered an adequate refutation of the underlying claim which itself, let it be stressed, is a fundamentally ethical one. Following Nietzsche, Foucault (1961/2006) argues for the extent to which seeming ethical advances resulting in the more compassionate treatment of the mentally ill can be interpreted as increasingly sophisticated methods of silencing abnormality in the interests of power.

Popular criticism of psychoanalysis often rests upon claims that treatment is unnecessarily lengthy, and that the profession is therefore fundamentally corrupt in allowing patients to suffer while more active approaches are claimed to deal with "the problem" more efficiently. In keeping with the extent to which the psychoanalytic method has traditionally been concerned with questions of resistance, Freud himself stresses that it is only to be expected that the field should find itself susceptible to widespread refutation. This tendency has of course been further emphasized by the big-money bureaucratization of the medical health-care system. As a consequence of the professional challenges thus arising, many analysts naturally feel impelled to adopt a revised attitude in relationship to the collective. However, in so far as public criticism of psychoanalysis may legitimately suggest a systemic resistance to change, there is also a clear danger that attempting to meet societal demand might significantly contravene the field's own core principles and commitments.[2]

Therapeutic footings

> The story of psychiatry began when one man attempted to relieve another man's suffering by influencing him.
>
> (Alexander & Selesnick, 1966, p. 17)

In seeking to provide his patient with the conditions to speak freely, Josef Breuer's response to the case of Anna O. remains radical. The possible implications for society underlying the seemingly innocuous gesture of privileging a patient's experience are far from having been absorbed. In the extent to which psychoanalysis has come to be regarded by the mainstream as archaic, the field has understandably sought to reform itself. Nevertheless, with the challenge that psychoanalytic discourse poses to established power structures, it might also be conceivable that the widespread dismissal of depth psychology is at least partially indicative of systemic resistances. In response to the profound authoritarianism of the American psychoanalytic mainstream during its heyday, recent decades have witnessed an understandable desire to shift the field's discourse towards a more open register of exchange – a tendency that has not only been necessary, but also to the unquestionable enrichment of practice. Nevertheless, an understandable concern remains that psychoanalysis grows estranged from its more radical basis when an emphasis comes to be placed on adaptation.

Foregrounding dialogue, the relational shift has implications not only for practice, but also for how psychoanalysis as a discipline attends to the claims made upon it by contemporary life – that is, the question of how the analyst listens to the analysand seems closely related to the question of how psychoanalysis as a discipline attends to the wider claims of society. In so far as an attitude of accommodation comes to be adopted in respect of societal demand, it can seem that the field is implicitly willing to accept its given diagnosis and position itself in the role of ailing patient. Under pressure from numerous forms of criticism, psychoanalysis is made to feel that it doesn't fit in – that its place in the established order has been cast in doubt. Psychoanalysts themselves suffer with the loss of professional prestige, a dwindling of opportunities to work, and a sense of not being understood by others. In light of all this, the field's survival seems dependent on its being able to evolve. At the same time, the necessary movement to address abuses of psychoanalytic power exposes the profession to another form of vulnerability; this being that psychoanalysis in the English-speaking world was developed and has survived on the basis of its relationship to medicine. Thus, the more hermeneutically nuanced psychoanalytic theorizing becomes, the more conflicted is the field's relationship to the scientific paradigm upon which its authority has historically depended.

The principal commitment of psychoanalysis is to the clinical situation itself, yet the clinical situation is only ethically tenable if the underlying theory of mind supporting it reflects this. Given the seeming incompatibility of the dialogic-relational ethos with the positivism of medical science, it might be argued that the profession's future depends on distancing itself from the mainstream and aligning more with the tropes of alternative medicine. While a move of this kind may in fact prove necessary, as long as psychoanalytic practice posits itself as a form of therapy intended for the treatment of individuals – whether explicitly designated as "patients" or otherwise – the challenges attendant to the question of authority remain. The extent to which constructivist thinking can reasonably be applied to the therapeutic relationship appears limited by virtue of the clinical situation itself, just as the extent to which therapeutic practice can claim to reflect a two-person approach to treatment is inevitably limited by the conditions defining treatment. Upon encountering these limits, it seems that either the constructivist line of thinking renders the psychoanalyst's profession theoretically untenable, or else this position has to be challenged or modified in order to establish a foundation for practice. Since psychoanalysis still posits itself as a therapy in the conventional sense, the fundamental asymmetry of the psychoanalytic relationship continues to be emphasized – were this recognition to be lost then the justification for treatment collapses. Yet for the therapeutic relationship's asymmetry to be justified the clinician most grant that he or she can assume a meaningful relationship to the question of clinical truth. Even if, following Loewald (1980), the effort to understand is deemed more primary than any question of presumed knowing, the idea of knowing is still implied in the professional credibility of the analyst's capacity to listen and discern meaning.

Placing to one side the obvious disciplinary problems raised in the clash between hermeneutic and scientific forms of discourse, it remains questionable whether medical psychiatry and/or clinical psychology still offer a sufficient basis for psychoanalysis to anchor itself. The extent to which the profession has come to be rejected in these quarters suggests not. Nor should this surprise us – put simply, an approach emphasizing the over-determination of meaning clearly stands opposed to the business of scientific fact-making. Efforts to minimize the uncertainty of psychology's inductive proofs continue to structure a discourse that is inherently exclusionary – academic psychology's lasting reliance on "nature versus nurture" is paradigmatic of this, with any attempt to question the suppositions of this basic frame of reference often immediately ridiculed as an example of magical thinking. The notion of over-determination suggests that psychoanalysis has always adopted an approach to the mind which is fundamentally incompatible with an emphasis on manifest pathology. A medical doctor has little need of taking a patient's perceptions into account when treating a broken leg, nor is the outcome of such a procedure likely to be much affected by the willingness of the physician to adopt a stance that would accommodate the patient's beliefs about the nature of the accident or its relationship to the analysand's life situation. With advances in neuroscience and the chemical suppression of mental illness, if psychoanalysis is to justify itself as anything more than an outmoded therapeutic lean-to, an assertion has to be made that the value and meaning of treatment extends beyond mere symptom relief. It is precisely at this point, however, that theory starts to lose its footing in medical practice:

> Moreover, if the concept of cure is more or less definable medically in terms of bodily or psycho-somatic standards, it is not so easily definable psychologically in so far as an essential element of psychological standards must necessarily include religious and philosophical considerations. When, for instance, a man suffering from difficulties of adaptation to life of a non-organic order undergoes a psycho-therapeutic treatment that leads to a better adaptation or cure, it can always be questioned in principle, either by philosophy or religion, whether such a cure has not been achieved at the price of a vitiation of attitude with respect to the values of the soul. It is not surprising therefore to note that medical investigators who fathered modern psychotherapy justified their extra-medical investigations in the name and authority of science in general rather than medicine in particular.
>
> (Christou, 1963, p. 3)

In the extent to which psychoanalytic practice continues to seek epistemic refuge in the seeming safe haven of medical discourse, the field's capacity to develop is correspondingly restricted. Thomas Szasz (1961) notoriously criticizes psychiatry and the classical approach to psychoanalysis precisely in claiming that these disciplines sacrifice truth in their desire to imitate medicine. Szasz argues that doctors should only be allowed to treat those diseases that can be proven as such with recourse to biology. This approach is in keeping with the tendency demonstrated in the early history of psychology which correlates an apparently inorganic disturbance with the possibility of a psychological cure. With scientific advance, however, Szasz's position becomes less helpful. Whether in calling for the de-pathologizing of mental illness or in supporting calls for psychosocial modalities of treatment, making a distinction between organic and inorganic pathologies has grown counter-productive. As a consequence of the historical role played by the discourse of the nature versus nurture distinction, the understandable outrage caused by such crudely expressed notions as the "schizophrenogenic mother" (Fromm-Reichmann, 1948) and the "refrigerator parent" (Kanner, 1949) are readily attacked on the basis of neurological or genetic signifiers, allowing the impression to be fostered that psychoanalysis has thus been disproven (e.g., Dolnick, 1998). Where the absence of organic "evidence" had once constituted a significant justification for non-reductive approaches to mental disturbance, this line of reasoning has now come to serve an opposing agenda.

Attitudes such as Szasz's become self-defeating in that they legitimize the notion that an affliction of the psyche can be "proven" with recourse to biology. In today's climate, it becomes ever more apparent that the distinction between mental and physical disturbance is not at all clear, having more to do with the question of an approach than it does with a clearcut either/or. Common sense now suggests that every mental illness is expressed in some respect by the body. Equally, we would be hard-pressed to think of a physical illness that does not have some bearing on the subjective experience of the person effected – we don't consider the common cold a mental illness, and yet as Winnicott (1966) suggests, the instance of such an affliction has clear implications for lived experience and may yet be responded to as such. With its distinction between medical and psychological interventions, the history of psychiatry has tended to reinforce the notion that these two methods of approach point to two distinct kinds of disturbance. As a consequence, clinicians find themselves functioning within a system that frequently attempts to cast judgment on whether a person's experience can be considered psychologically meaningful. That this state of affairs is so widely accepted has disturbing implications. The insufficiency of the nature versus nurture debate lies in the extent to which the terms of the conversation have been fundamentally skewed towards a set of assumptions that privilege the established order. In considering that individual differences are always determined by material causes (whether biological or social), the subject's experience is implicitly drained of meaning, with whatever value might be imputed to this experience only being registered in terms of the system as it stands.

Materialism unexamined

> I believe that we are witness either to the emergence of a new emphasis within personal illness or we are just getting around to perceiving an element in personality that has always been with us. This element is a particular drive to be normal, one that is typified by the numbing and eventual erasure of subjectivity, in favour of a self that is conceived as a material object among other man-made products in the object world.
>
> (Bollas, 1987, p. 135)

Efforts within the American academic tradition to establish psychology along conventionally scientific lines have naturally resulted in the widespread adoption of a physicalist paradigm (Taylor, 1985, p. 119). This tendency was prompted by behaviorists in their effort to exclude the study of mental states from the very field ostensibly established to examine them, and is evidenced in the present day with the dominance of neuroscience. Within psychoanalysis, the professional necessity of maintaining some claim to authority has ensured that while contemporary theory has drawn heavily from hermeneutics, the field has by no means surrendered its attachment to science and the medical mainstream. The point of contact between these two strands of discourse has tended to be construed in the experience of the body, and it is the essentialism associated with this notion that relational theory has been most reticent to sacrifice.

Mitchell and Aron (1999) state: "In their emancipatory zeal to shed social impositions, more political forms of constructivism seem not to appreciate that we are what we have been, and that we construct ourselves out of the materials at hand, including our bodies and their attributes" (p. xvi). While a significant issue has been raised here, the position taken might be challenged in seeking to establish how we interpret the "materials at hand." For Mitchell and Aron, these materials are construed in terms of material reality as reflected in the fact of our bodies. In adopting this position, the constructivist paradigm is seemingly abandoned in favor of endorsing a metaphysical claim concerning the primacy of matter. Mitchell and Aron propose a form of relational thinking that allows a place for "the materiality of the body and its attributes" (p. xvi), while suggesting that the fashion in which we describe this material reality is inevitably constructed. By adopting an attitude that we can, on the basis of what seems reasonable, pick and choose between constructs and facts, the constructivist and materialist paradigms are in danger of being allied merely to protect basic assumptions. We have seen that this approach to constructivism is reminiscent of Searle (1998), who likewise suggests that there are two kinds of facts: those that are independent of human observers, and those that require consensual agreement. It might be noted that although Searle intended his approach to constructivism as a major contribution that would bridge the discourses of continental and analytic philosophy, the muted critical response this work received may be considered indicative of the extent to which Searle fails to seriously engage the claims of the latter. It has even been argued that Searle's basic approach is in effect merely a recapitulation of the much earlier work of Emile Durkheim (Gross, 2006) – one of the major figures from the world of sociology that constructivist thinking arose in opposition to. In seeking to posit a distinction between constructed truth and material fact, a position like Searle's comes to reflect nothing more than the basic commitments of a philosophical materialism only moderately informed by constructivist thinking. Attitudes of this kind also contribute to the fallacious notion that a wholeheartedly constructivist standpoint necessarily seeks to undermine the "reality" of our assumed truths, yet such a claim only seems legitimate if we continue to think in the terms of the paradigm being challenged.

The question of authenticity raised in respect to constructivist thinking is even reinforced at the level of language itself – consider the distinction between *natural* science and social *construct*. Donnel Stern (1997) writes: "Reality is a social construction, though it feels so familiar and inevitable that we can scarcely believe it is anything other than natural" (p. 8). That the notion of social construction is conceived by Stern as *unnatural* indicates that the constructivist position is still being measured against the terms of positivism. In a related sense, Donna Orange believes that postulating truth as a construct is commensurate with the idea that we can know nothing of the human condition. With this in mind, she commits to a form of realism that allows for the pursuit of an "ever-more-adequate conception of human nature" (Orange, 1995, p. 29) that will provide a "positive account of what constitutes scientific progress [and] psychoanalytic cure" (Orange, 1992, p. 562). A more thoroughgoing constructivism pointing towards a participatory outlook might suggest that human nature is itself constantly emerging (nature as a shape-shifter), perhaps finding support in Schelling's (1799/2004) contention that "to philosophize about nature means to create nature" (p. 14).

The extent to which most relational thinking can properly consider itself to have broken free of the basic assumptions of positivism is clearly questionable. Ironically, in distinction to the weak-form constructivism/perspectivism typically favored by relationalists, Boudry and Buekens (2011) argue against the classical psychoanalytic paradigm precisely on the basis that they see Freud's thinking as an example of strong-form constructivism. In this light, we might wonder whether the postmodern turn in psychoanalysis has in fact witnessed the theorizing of postmodernity modified to such an extent that contemporary theorizing is more "classical" in its outlook than the work of Freud – while Freud argued from a professedly scientific sensibility for a position that was often radical in its implications, contemporary relational thinking tends to adopt postmodern theory in support of an underlying position funda-mentally rooted in philosophical materialism. Nissim-Sabat (2005) has drawn attention to the dangers of adopting such a position:

> Now, if a therapist believes, consciously or unconsciously, that physicality is what is real and all that falls under the rubric of "subjective" is reducible to phy-sicality, might not this belief compromise the therapist's ability to appreciate, to empathize with, this client's suffering? If one believes that subjectivity is reducible to, is really only "matter," if the subject who experiences feelings is "really" only a thing, can one thing connect intersubjectively with another thing? If feelings are naturalized, are they any longer feelings? Can one reified, dehumanized "subject" connect or empathize with another? What is there to empathize with?
> (p. 210)

The implications for psychoanalytic practice where the unconscious is portrayed as a relational construct conceived against a background of materialist presupposition are profound. Such a position has an obvious allure in that it coincides so readily with the assumptions of mainstream psychiatry and the broader commitments of the scientific worldview. For Searle (1994),[3] who is critical in his response to Freud's work, the nature of the unconscious can be defined only as: "the ontology of a neurophysiology capable of generating the conscious" (p. 172). In response to this statement, Chessick (2001) claims that Freud only speaks of unconscious processes *as if* they were already mental, and to read him otherwise is a distortion (p. 671). On this basis, Chessick suggests that Freud's position might be a good deal more compatible with Searle than Searle himself realizes. Spezzano (1996a) concurs, claiming that Freud implies as much as Searle makes explicit in positing consciousness as "an inherent biological property of the nervous system" (p. 608).

While there may be some substance to these claims, such arguments might be criticized for not adequately recognizing the extent to which Freud's psychology, despite its ties to neurology, does in practice distance itself from biology. Reflecting a participatory perspective, a more radical response might go further, and point out that the claim that consciousness is entirely dependent on the activity of the brain is itself an unproven assumption. In keeping with this, Rosenbaum (2012) has set forth a distinction between consciousness of which we are conscious and consciousness of which we are unconscious. She justifies the seemingly bizarre idea that consciousness is still present even when we are – according to all neurological markers – unconscious, by citing studies that indicate how individuals under deep anesthesia or in cardiac arrest have subsequently been able to recall impressions of events taking place in the operating room (p. 273). Similarly, while recognizing the extent to which the phenomenology of the mind is clearly linked with the functioning of the brain, transpersonal theorist Stanislav Grof (1992) observes that the assumption of consciousness having its origin in the brain is a metaphysical article of faith, and not a proven scientific fact.[4] In portraying his own point of view, he offers the following analogy:

> A good television repair person can look at the particular distortion of the picture or sound of a television set and tell us exactly what is wrong with it and which parts must be replaced to make it work properly again. No one would see this as proof that the set itself was responsible for the programs we see when we turn it on.
>
> (Grof, 1992, p. 5)[5]

Contrary to Chessick (2001) and Spezzano's (1996) claims that the Freudian unconscious is basically compatible with Searle's apparent objection to it, Freud's (1900) statement that the unconscious constitutes the "true psychical reality" (p. 613) is explicit in insisting upon a psychological bedrock as the proper basis for approaching psychic life, and not one that is to be reduced to the chemistry of the brain. While Freud never seems to have lost hope that his theories might eventually be corroborated by neuroscience, his approach to the mind is nonetheless largely a psychological one. By contrast, Searle's (1994) significant claim that consciousness is ontologically subjective seems not to have penetrated the substance of his own thinking. In his concern to avoid slipping into idealism, Searle in fact states that the distinction he draws between intrinsic intentionality (that which is attributed to "true" mental states) and as-if intentionality (that which only gives the impression of being intentional without, it is claimed, being so) is necessary since "the price of giving it up would be that everything would become mental" (p. 156). In keeping with a metaphysical commitment to avoid such an outcome, Searle claims that attributions to the unconscious are not intended to be taken metaphorically; that they "lose their explanatory power if we do not take them literally" (p. 156), by which he apparently intends, as a material fact.

Not considering that what a person experiences as "literal" might itself be subjectively determined, Searle posits his own assumptions as universally binding and proceeds on the basis that "literally" can only mean having intrinsic intentionality which, by his line of reasoning, comes to mean being objectively true on the basis of neurophysiology. But if consciousness is considered ontologically subjective, it seems entirely inconsistent to contend that the explanatory power of the unconscious rests upon its being regarded as objectively valid. While emergence theory appears to offer the promise of providing a scientific basis for what Freeman (2003) dubs "nonreductive physicalism," the scientific groundedness of this approach would seem to rest upon ignoring that the emergent property [consciousness] of the system subtending it [the brain] is the very medium by which the system subtending it comes to be postulated as such in the first place. Searle's (2002) vigorous resistance to being labeled a property dualist is indicative of an attempt to stave off the metaphysical challenges that clearly threaten when an emergentist position is taken on the phenomenon of consciousness. It is precisely these challenges that must be more directly confronted if contemporary psychoanalysis is to avoid coming to the same kind of theoretical impasse evidenced previously in the mid-twentieth-century stultification of the classical mainstream.

As a consequence of the limited extent to which relational thinking has actually embraced a constructivist standpoint, contemporary relational analysis can sometimes be criticized for the very essentialism it appears to refute. Mitchell (2000) argues that any anti-essentialist critique of relational theory's universalizing claims as to the constructed nature of mind is by definition invalid, since the notion of cultural relativism seemingly depends upon a universal claim concerning the relational nature of mind: "thus the postmodern critique of relationality as universal and fundamental depends upon the presumption of relationality as universal and fundamental" (p. xiii). This defense misses the point, since a thoroughgoing anti-essentialist response to relational theorizing is far more likely to find fault with Mitchell's position in respect of matter and the body, than engage in the kind of argument Mitchell imputes. Mitchell vocalizes his commitment to a social constructivist paradigm while implicitly endorsing a more comprehensive commitment to philosophical materialism. In so far as this outlook can be considered broadly reflected in relational thinking, the failure to more wholeheartedly pursue a constructivist point of view perhaps suggests the extent to which recent theorizing has failed to uphold the primacy of the individual's experience.

Constructivism's intellectual roots can be traced to the subjective idealism of Berkeley and Vico (Zepf et al., 2007, p. 7) – an intellectual current with strong links to the Germanic idealism that gave rise to the notion of the unconscious in the first place. Schelling (1800/1993) originally gives voice to the philosophical idea of the unconscious partly in response to Fichte's rejection of the Kantian thing-in-itself. Based on Kant's observation that the principles of cause and effect are only applicable in terms of the *phenomena*, Fichte reasons that the *noumena* cannot be the cause of the *phenomena*. On this basis Fichte states that consciousness is not grounded in anything outside of itself, thus potentially doing away with the notion of a *noumenal* world beyond our immediate comprehension. Schelling felt that Fichte's philosophy moved too far towards subjective idealism and had regrettably divorced itself from the aesthetic approach to nature outlined in Kant's *Critique of Judgement*. His solution was to assert an *indifference* between the subject and the object – one that preserves both the question of sameness and difference (Seidel, 2010, pp. 184–185). In this regard, Sherman (2008) suggests that Schelling's work can be read partly as a response to Spinozan pantheism, wherein the notion of participation is taken to such an extreme that the distinction between creator and created is effectively collapsed, undermining the concept of participation itself and resulting in a mechanistic fatalism.

Thus Schelling seeks to avert the apparent dangers of Kantian skepticism, Fichtean solipsism, and Spinozan determinism, by suggesting that the Absolute itself be considered as a creative subject; a subject in relationship to which humanity exceeds itself by actively participating in its becoming. In taking this position, Schelling comes to formulate the philosophical basis for a psychology of the unconscious. The emergence of the philosophical idea of the unconscious can therefore be considered a reaction to the threat of solipsism implied by the proto-constructivist philosophy of subjective idealism – a solution which, in retaining the notion of the self as primary, is altogether different from the approach of contemporary psychoanalysis wherever it asserts the primacy of the material world. This contemporary commitment of faith in the metaphysical postulate of matter is, of course, in and of itself quite defensible, yet it is critical that this commitment be recognized as faith-based and not clinically necessary. Furthermore, it is surely questionable to what extent a position with such restrictive implications for the notion of subjectivity can really be considered compatible with an approach to clinical practice that emphasizes the question of pluralism. To make this observation is not to argue for or against the final truth of the materialist standpoint, but simply to demonstrate the extent to which an underlying worldview of this kind might be implicated in clinical practice such as to contravene working ideals.

First principles

> Every scientific man in order to preserve his reputation has to say he dislikes metaphysics. What he means is he dislikes having his metaphysics criticized.
>
> (Whitehead, 1927)[6]

In an extended engagement with the participatory philosophy of Schelling, McGrath (2012) suggests that emphasizing clinical or statistical primacy in an attempt to rescue depth psychology from its metaphysical presuppositions may be shortsightedly restrictive. He seeks to offer an alternative:

Another option is to follow the immanent logic of depth psychology and make its crypto-metaphysics explicit, perhaps even to improve it, not by more precise accommodation to clinical results, but by creating more adequate speculative concepts. This is what the Schelling school ventured with respect to the medical psychology of their day [...] not to deduce metaphysical principles from empirical results or hypothesize metaphysical structure only insofar as the empirical results warrant the hypothesis, but rather to fuse the a priori and the a posteriori element in psychology and approach the empirical through the metaphysical. This approach is still valid, however unpopular it might be in psychology departments. A speculative psychology would not grant empirical psychology its presumed metaphysical neutrality; on the contrary. The implicit metaphysics of empirical psychology (by and large Cartesianism) would be exposed and deconstructed, a critique that would happen on not only historical, but also explicitly metaphysical terrain.

(p. 20)

Although avowedly pragmatic in its outlook, the field of mental health care is nevertheless founded in theoretical assumption. For many helping professionals, examining the nature of these assumptions can seem ancillary to practice. For contemporary psychoanalysis, however, doing so must be considered fundamental. The apparent rite of passage reflected in the training analysis is intended to ensure that every psychoanalytic practitioner broaches the question of what draws them to the field. Engaging this subject is clearly important if the clinician is to be mindful of the extent to which his or her own needs are implicated in their desire to work with others. Equally significant, however, is how we conceptualize the purpose of the work itself. In so far as this question is more obviously theoretical, the response to it has traditionally been secured by way of institutional authority rather than by looking to the clinician's own values. The shift towards a more pluralistic approach to theory, however, is inevitably changing this. In so doing, a considerable challenge is posed. While theoretical pluralism might act as an inducement for the practitioner to more carefully examine their own basis in theory, the intellectual demand thus implied can also result in an avoidance of the question.

This tendency is exacerbated with the privileging *in* theory of practice *over* theory, as expressed in the language of what, following Kohut (1977), is often referred to as "experience near" thinking (a remnant of positivism), alongside the notion that we can freely "choose" our theories on the basis of what seems clinically useful. With precedents in Anna Freud's (1946) therapeutically driven attitude towards theory building and Heinz Hartmann's (1939) social psychology approach to the definition of mental health, positions of this kind tend to rely on an insufficiently problematized relationship to the mainstream clinical paradigm. Only in taking for granted the assumptions of this paradigm can the conditions be established for whatever "experience" the analyst presumes nearness to. Similarly, if a theoretically justified approach to the analysand is to be deemed clinically useful without recourse to the theoretical system in question, the terms indicating a theory's adequacy are liable to be defined by the unchallenged theoretical authority of the clinical situation itself. While an immense benefit has been gleaned from focusing on the mechanics of relational exchange, analyst and analysand are also both unavoidably grand theorists – a refusal to pay service to this question reflects an unwillingness to examine first principles. The contemporary clinician must therefore remain committed to engage with what is ultimately intended by analyzing, so that bottom-up approaches to practice are recognized to exist in tension with thinking from the top-down.

Efforts to embrace theoretical inclusivity remain a work in progress, with the limits of this endeavor drawing attention to the exclusionary presuppositions of the field at present. An early attempt to bridge disparate strands of psychoanalytic thought was undertaken by Stolorow and Atwood (1979). Their initial approach, while noteworthy in its breadth of influence, is undermined by a philosophically limited methodology which belies the work's apparent goal – an outlook that has subsequently been revised by the authors, with this shift conceptualized by them as a movement from phenomenology to phenomenological contextualism (Atwood Stolorow, 2014). In their earlier work, Stolorow and Atwood (1979) claim that the proliferation of psychoanalytic theories should be moderated by a set of principles intended to adjudicate their relative values. The authors' reliance on their own totalizing ideals, however, inevitably renders this project suspect: "Our thesis is that the continuing progress of the field will depend upon the clarification of limiting subjective influences in theory building and on the elaboration of concepts and methods belonging to a level of generality higher than that hitherto attained" (p. 6). This professed concern for interrogating theoretical subjectivity does not extend to the authors adequately recognizing the subjectivity of their own endeavor. The very concern that the early Stolorow and Atwood have for founding assumptions is not sufficiently recognized as itself resting on its own set of beliefs, and the authors therefore appear to imply that they can get clear of their own position.

With Atwood and Stolorow's more recent emphasis on context, this attitude has been refined. Drawing from the hermeneutics of Gadamer, Stolorow (2003) now seeks to emphasize the ontological role of interpretation so that the "dichotomy between interpreting and relating collapses" (p. 221). In endorsing Orange's notion of perspectival realism (Stolorow et al., 2002, Chapter 6), however, Stolorow continues to assume that the implications of subjectivity are restricted to the domain of persons, thus positing a form of realism that implies a harmonious and stable background to our contextually dependent experience. While Stolorow (2011) states that the allure of metaphysics is a reflection of the fear of human finitude, this possibly reductive statement in itself reflects a foundational truth claim. In their most recently revised work, Atwood and Stolorow (2014) state: "A truly *psychoanalytic* phenomenology resists the philosopher's temptation to define consciousness in universal terms and instead seeks understanding of the phenomena transpiring in the specific intersubjective dialogue of the psychoanalytic situation" (p. 26). The authors claim a distinction between what they term "emotional phenomenology" and metaphysics – the former is portrayed as transient yet real, while the latter is merely an illusion. The profoundly problematic nature of this distinction is such that even the authors themselves finally come to concede that they can't avoid imposing their own metaphysics, yet in light of this recognition their professed response is to recommend a constant reflection on the contexts for our ideas "including the idea of context itself" (p. 140). The result of contextualizing context, however, would surely be to recognize that this kind of contextualism is only one way of structuring our worldview.[7]

Adopting a different approach to the question of theoretical pluralism, in *Drive, Ego, Object and Self: A Synthesis for Clinical Work*, contemporary Freudian analyst Fred Pine (1990) compares and contrasts what he perceives to be the four major motivational theories of mainstream thinking. Pine's approach is unabashedly pragmatic, and as such he is satisfied to construct an argument that each theory of motivation can be shown to have its own clinical uses. Since Pine does not attempt to reconcile theoretical differences his attitude might be commended for its modesty, yet criticized for its lack of engagement with the underlying conflicts.[8] He writes:

> To aim in this direction [...] is not necessarily to aim for an integration of the various theories themselves. [...] all carry a lot of metapsychological baggage; and it is not my aim to pull all of that together. But each of the theories does highlight particular aspects of the substantive *phenomena* of human functioning, and I shall endeavor to develop a view which gives place to all of them.
>
> (Pine, 1990, p. 8)

Pine shares Stolorow and Atwood's (1979) tendency to dismiss that which is not readily amenable to clinical synthesis as "metapsychology" – a term which has not infrequently come to assume derisive undertones, and has its origins in Freud's bid to artificially separate psychoanalysis from philosophy (Frie & Reis, 2005, p. 5). In keeping with some of Stolorow's (2003) more recent observations, however, we might ask to what extent the clinical phenomena a theory claims to identify can really be rendered distinct from the theory itself. The idea that "experiential facts" are separable from the theoretical constructs we use to interpret them is clearly questionable. Our conceptions about the world, which find expression in our theories, precede and give shape to what we experience as the facts. Failure to properly credit this can only be expected to further limit clinical receptivity. In her recent work, Donna Orange (2011) has returned to Ricoeur's (1970) distinction between a hermeneutics of suspicion and one of faith/trust, arguing that the field's future is best served by emphasizing the latter. Privileging trust over suspicion might seem a self-evident gesture in the direction of what Orange terms "clinical hospitality," but this notion of trust ultimately rests on a perception of *things as they seem* that can just as readily annul the other as affirm them. While the notion of analytic suspicion can no doubt be abused, the very same can be said of trust. Clinicians cannot afford, therefore, to privilege one mode of listening over the other, nor choose selectively (in keeping, that is, with a perception of "the facts") which ear to listen with when.

The often encountered aversion to so-called metapsychology threatens to reflect a lack of concern for basic assumptions. Justified on the basis of *doing what works for the patient*, this apparent short-cut to clinical liberation can, in practice, culminate in blinkered thinking. No doubt such a strategy is in keeping with the academic vogue as expressed in the recent history of the humanities and social sciences, where post-structuralist influence contextualized in Anglo-American pragmatism has led to a presumed throwing-out of metaphysics in favor of an allegedly more rigorous and less exclusionary epistemology. The trouble, however, is that a metaphysics is necessarily implied in all discourse. Greenberg and Mitchell (1983) point to this quite categorically where they indicate that all psychoanalytic theories reflect metaphysical commitments (p. 382). While strongly emphasizing the inherently conflictual nature of psychodynamic theorizing – they dismiss mixed mode approaches as "unstable and at times contrived" (p. 380) – what the authors do not always fully credit is that commitments of this kind are made in the sub-stance of our encounter with the analysand, and not simply after the fact in the mere application of theory to case material. Similarly, Benjamin (2010) asserts that "people choose the theories that fit themselves" (p. 112) – a position which she ascribes also to the "perspectivist school" of Aron (1996) and Hoffman (1998). This outlook is considerably more nuanced than the idea that theories should simply be chosen on the basis of the results they yield, yet it remains necessary to avoid making the mistake of introducing an artificial split between the analyst's person-ality and its expression by way of theory. Greenberg and Mitchell (1983) write: "Although the practicing psychoanalyst attempts to suspend his formal theoretical preconceptions as he listens to his analysands, to stay as close as possible to the phenomenology of the analysand's experience, theory must enter at some point" (p. 15). To propose that theory enters is misleading. Psychoanalytic thought, in so far as it reflects an expression of the analyst's own subjectivity, manifests in a living experience of the other. Theory doesn't enter (it cannot simply be bracketed out with recourse to an evenly suspended attention), but is to a considerable extent present from the outset. Claiming that our clinical interactions can in some sense get clear of theory is only true in a limited sense – that is, in the extent to which the theory in question is not an immediate expression of the analyst's lived experience.

In a later text, addressing the emergence of the relational trend, Mitchell (1993) outlines another kind of distinction:

> This shift in thinking has taken place not on the level of theory but on the level of metatheory: theory about theory. It does not concern questions about what motivates the analysand, the structure of the mind, the development of emotional life. Rather, it concerns the question of what the analyst can know about any of these things. This realm of current psychoanalytic debate entails a fundamental redefinition of the very nature of psychoanalytic thought and psychoanalysis as a discipline.
>
> (p. 42)

In a footnote to this paragraph, Mitchell concedes that the line he draws between theory and metatheory is in practice not so clear cut. He states that this distinction might nevertheless be considered a "heuristic device" to help explore recent shifts in discourse. It might be asked whether this approach can really be considered heuristic, or is more simply a distortion. Whether speaking of metatheory or metapsychology, introducing an artificial break in our conceptualizations of the clinical situation can be misleading.

It should be clear that the very notion of metapsychology is somewhat peculiar. The designation is introduced to draw a line between the supposed empirically given "facts" of psychology, and the systems we use to try and explain them. But to even obtain the sense of having grasped something approximating a fact, a whole system of interpretation needs to be established beforehand. If "psychology" is a term used to signify the human subject's attempts to make a systematic object of study out of the human subject, in a significant sense *all psychology is metapsychology* in so far as it would seek to theoretically encapsulate lived experience in language. In attempting to reject or gain distance from so-called metapsychology, the most immediate consequence is only to more directly reify that which is allowed to remain in discourse by virtue of its status as supposedly distinct experiential fact.

The intent to provide more room for exchange by being less dogmatic only suppresses fundamentals, thus obstructing the creative vitality of an ongoing conversation between theories of the personality wherein divergent opinions help elucidate and challenge our underlying assumptions. In response to Levenson's (1992) contention that psychoanalysis should be conceived purely as a methodology so that different theoretical models might be applied *within* this setting, we might note that theory is inevitably present from the outset not only in terms of the two individuals approaching the treatment, but also in the very constellation of the therapeutic relationship itself. The tendency to dismiss those forms of psychoanalytic theorizing that are not immediately grounded in clinical material can insidiously lead to a climate of anti-intellectualism that functions to protect biases. Donnel Stern (2009) argues that while genuine intellectual innovation is always guided by affect, the sense of duty to defend our preferred theorists leads to a psychoanalytic parochialism that has, in the field's more recent history, culminated in a denigration of ideas expressed institutionally as a foregrounding of the importance of feelings to the exclusion of thought (p. 302). Stern's (1991) own approach might unwittingly exacerbate this tendency, however, where he claims "common human influences" (p. 75) are closer to immediate experience than our theoretical commitments.

If the basis for all utterance resides in something unresolved, there may be a fundamental tendency towards splitting implicit in all discourse. Thus, assuming *any* position implies conflict and contradiction. New life requires an environment in which to prosper, and the aversion to first principles is not always conducive to establishing an incubatory space in discourse – emerging ideas need some measure of push-back against which to test and define themselves. Where clinicians in effect seek to justify their position by claiming not to offer final justifications, an attempt is registered to evade the conflict. As the Heraclitean maxim states: *all things come into being through strife necessarily*. Paul Ricoeur (1970) writes:

> In general terms, every *mythos* involves a latent *logos* which demands to be exhibited. That is why there are no symbols without the beginning of interpretation; where one man dreams, prophesies, or poetizes, another rises up to interpret. Interpretation organically belongs to symbolic thought and its double meaning.
>
> (p. 19)

Where the myth of the clinical situation (and all of the tropes associated with it) goes insufficiently recognized as such, the *logos* functions less consciously and thus grows all the more absolutist. This is the inevitable consequence of too aggressively seeking to pursue professional credibility, as expressed in the widespread recourse to pragmatism. In ostensibly attempting to avoid conflict by emphasizing a false distinction between clinical data and our ideas about it, contemporary psychoanalysis literalizes the underlying assumptions of the clinical framework. While these assumptions cannot be abandoned entirely, neither can we afford to lose sight of them by relying too heavily on the dictates of practicality.

Cure and credibility

> Psychoanalysis began as therapy, its knowledge comes from that source and psychotherapy according to its nature must be oriented morally or at least normatively. Whether it has to do with the medical concept of normality or with the social concept of adaptation, therapy can never be without prejudice for it sets out from the standpoint that something should be otherwise than it is, no matter how one might formulate it.
>
> (Rank, 1936, p. 14)

As addressed most explicitly in *The Question of Lay Analysis*, Freud (1926) was unambiguously opposed to having psychoanalysis develop within a strictly medical context. Nonetheless, that the profession came to be associated so directly with medicine clearly served it well. From the mid-1930s until the return to a Kraepelinian system of diagnosis heralded by the publication of the DSM-III in 1980, psychodynamic thinking attained to what now seems an improbable degree of mainstream credibility. While psychoanalysis was practiced within the context of medical psychiatry, the fundamentally uncertain nature of the profession was outwardly minimized. With the steady erosion of psychoanalytic thinking's mainstream respectability, however, the field's ambiguous nature has ceased to suggest merely theoretical concerns and has come to reflect basic questions of survival.

One of the most obvious problems facing psychoanalysis at the present time pertains to how the profession is to interface with a scientific milieu which, for numerous reasons, is finding psychoanalytic theory ever more unacceptable. Nor does the battle for this kind of respect seem all that contestable. This claim can be made not on the basis of a feeling about what psychoanalysis should or shouldn't be, but merely with an eye for the terms of the conflict – put simply, the profession must contend with the stark fact that the pharmaceutical and insurance industries are two of the most profitable in the United States. The control that these industries might therefore be assumed to exert over legislation is significant. In addition, clinical studies are more often than not financed by these same private interests in the expectation that the results garnered will serve their needs; should they happen not to, the funding party is at liberty to have the outcome presented selectively, or else withheld from being made public altogether. Whitaker (2010) has drawn attention to the inestimable impact of the for-profit clinical drug trials industry that emerged in the late 1980s. Clearly research of this kind is completely antithetical to scientific pretensions of bias elimination. Whitaker cites the following passage from an article published in the *New England Journal of Medicine*:

> The ties between clinical researchers and industry include not only grant support, but also a host of other financial arrangements. Researchers also serve as consultants to companies whose products they are studying, join advisory boards and speakers' bureaus, enter into patent and royalty arrangements, agree to be the listed authors of articles ghostwritten by interested companies, promote drugs and devices at company-sponsored symposiums, and allow themselves to be plied with expensive gifts and trips to luxurious settings. Many also have equity interests in the companies.
>
> (Angell, 2000, p. 264)

To an increasing extent, therapy's role is now to support the agenda of this industry in the task of stabilizing service users on medication. Meanwhile, the mainstream media encourages the public to demand "evidence-based" approaches from prospective therapists (e.g., Brown, 2013). The common-sense appeal that this kind of rhetoric plays to is clearly of no small account. Considered in this light, we might be more cautious in celebrating the notion that the classical position has been challenged by "critical consumerism" (Modell, 1991, p. 19). Without even attending to the question of whether the efficacy of psychoanalytic methods can be proven under the conditions that such a proof is expected to be met, the quest for psychoanalytic justification might still inevitably be consigned to failure in that the field simply doesn't have the financial influence to compete with the forces of the market. Given a realistic attitude towards the conflict it becomes apparent that, barring a major cultural upheaval, the decline of psychoanalytic respectability within medical circles can only be expected to continue.

The question, then, is not whether psychoanalysis can reverse the trend, but whether the field's future is best served in fighting a losing battle. Although this fight might still be contested while maneuvering for a long-term means of survival, it remains open to question whether the field's interests might thus be damaged in compromising on principles. Additionally, if in being more receptive to the influence not only of relational schools of thinking, but also to Lacanian, Jungian, and transpersonal approaches, psychoanalysis were to focus less on symptom relief and instead position itself more explicitly as a possible means towards living more creatively, the profession seems liable to jeopardize itself all the more categorically in terms of its original position vis-à-vis mainstream psychiatry. Embracing a more progressive position would likely hasten the demise of psychodynamic treatment in relationship to solutions-focused financial interests. On the other hand, an adjustment in emphasis might allow the field to reach out more directly to a different kind of sensibility – perhaps even enabling a much-needed revitalization of the profession's public image.

Clearly if analysts are to be at least semi-cognizant of the myriad ways in which they implicitly dictate to the beliefs of analysands, it is imperative that clinicians remain mindful of how they locate themselves in respect to the apparent evolution of the clinical situation. With the extent to which the strictures of this situation have come to threaten psychoanalytic practice, this need seems to grow only more pressing. In profound contrast to the increasing demand for results, Freud stresses a belief that the analyst should carry out his or her work without concern for the effect it produces upon the perception of others:

> Under present-day conditions, the feeling that is most dangerous to a psychoanalyst is the therapeutic ambition to achieve by this novel and much disputed method something that will produce a convincing effect upon other people. This will not only put him into a state of mind which is unfavorable for his work, but will make him helpless against certain resistances of the analysand, whose recovery, as we know, primarily depends on the interplay of forces in him.
>
> (Freud, 1912, p. 115)

While the one-person model endorsed here can of course be made subject to significant criticism, the underlying ethical force of Freud's commitment to the patient continues to warrant attention. Freud appears to suggest that focusing on the notion of a consensually validated cure is liable to result in the individual's interests being sacrificed to the collective – the question of cure comes to be fetishized such that the "cured patient" merely reflects an object of the analyst's narcissism. Taking this perceived danger seriously, the clinician must always remain wary of dictating their own wishes to the analysand, even (and perhaps especially) if what they would want is the very thing they have been professionally engaged to accomplish – that is, the analysand's recovery. If a relational approach to psychotherapy is to attempt to ameliorate the dangers of dictating to the patient, it seems necessary that what is most unique and irreducible about the patient be considered the primary concern of treatment – a question of alterity which, owing to its emergent quality, neither analyst nor analysand can expect to define ahead of time nor incorporate into any treatment plan. Clearly a position of this kind cannot readily be translated into the terms of a recovery from illness.

The insistence upon results is expressive of a sensibility which implicitly considers people as means rather than ends. In contrast to the ways in which psychoanalysis in the English-speaking world has sought to retain contact with the medical paradigm, French psychoanalysis has been fundamentally shaped by Lacan's skepticism of cure. This skepticism expresses Freud's (1923c) insistence that recovery be treated as a byproduct of the analysis rather than its aim (p. 251). In refutation of the idea that the analyst should be guided by the intention of healing, Lacan (1966/2005) states unequivocally that "there is no other criterion of cure than the complete adoption by the subject of [the analyst's] measure" (p. 353). Similarly, Bion (1967) argues that it is impossible to directly desire a patient's development (p. 189); that thinking in terms of improvement indicates practice has been restricted in the name of the collective (p. 195); and that the notion of cure is a means of policing psychoanalysis thus "rendering it harmless to the Establishment" (Bion, 1970, p. 288). In keeping with these ideas, Žižek argues that under the conditions of advanced capitalism the aim of psychoanalysis has effectively been reversed – while treatment was once concerned with lifting social injunctions so as to help patients experience those forms of pleasure that were being denied them, at the present time psychoanalytic practice remains necessary precisely as a means to lifting the ideological injunction to "enjoy" (Wright, 2004). If a question of adaptation is still apparent here, then it manifests in terms of individuals adapting to *themselves* despite the world, rather than the opposite position which is the natural expression of pragmatism. An outlook of this more radical kind reflects an ethical impetus that through treatment the analysand should grow more able to endure the conditions of their own subjectivity – an ideal which is in stark contrast to the notion of symptom remission. This approach is clearly reflective of Žižek's Lacanian sensibilities, expressing the idea that pathological formations "have the dignity of fundamental philosophical attitudes towards reality" (Žižek, 2007, p. 4). James Hillman (1978) has similarly emphasized the creative potential of mental illness:

> In other words, every pathological bias obstructs the possibility of metaphysical instruction; once experiences have been labeled and declared abnormal, we cannot learn from them or let them carry us beyond their immediate actuality. They are trapped by their names into mechanical performance. They lose their flight of fantasy. So, indeed, we want to rid ourselves of such symptoms, which are not the symptoms so much as the names. From them we truly suffer; whereas the phenomena themselves, freed from their labels, become modes of unusual experience.
>
> (p. 146)

Hillman seeks to value psychopathological phenomena for their revelatory character, the undergoing of which is ultimately posited to result in a deepening of experience in respect to the question of death (Hillman, 1983, p. 51). Thus a reversal appears to take place and, rather than normalizing to the expectations of the social world, Hillman's approach normalizes against the normative so as to bring the analysand into a more direct relationship with the question of their own mortality.

Suggesting the underlying influence of Heidegger, there is a resonance between Lacan and Hillman's distinctive attitudes towards psychopathology, and the sensibilities of the existential psychotherapy movement. Rollo May (1958a) claims that this movement stands for "defining neurosis in terms of what destroys man's capacity to fulfill his own being" (p. 35). For existentialism, the notion of bad faith becomes the yardstick against which psychopathology is defined. Certain symptoms usually considered morbid are re-conceived as healthy, while some tendencies conventionally deemed healthy are now regarded as pathological; Medard Boss, for example, endorses encouraging patients to recognize guilt as an authentic experience rather than minimizing these feelings as merely indicative of neuroticism (May, 1958b, p. 54), while Abraham Maslow (1970) observes that the phenomenon of boredom may qualify as a pathology that the present age fails to acknowledge. Claims of this kind reflect a robust challenge to commonplace diagnostic assumptions. At the same time, these claims might also be considered an implicit warning, in that they indicate how readily an approach ostensibly concerned with validating the individual can come to establish its own norms.

Moving forwards?

> The concept of illness means that another principle, a foreign idea, asserts itself in the organism alongside the life idea. It thus hinders and disturbs the organism's life. The possibility for such a disturbance presupposes that the organism has some freedom to deviate from its original way of life; it is no longer determined by iron necessity [...] The disposition for illness increases in proportion to the growth of consciousness, and thus of freedom.
>
> (Carus, 1846/1989, p. 68)

In so far as the relational movement has been centrally concerned to embrace pluralism by questioning the notion of the analyst's authority, this movement has come to hint at an as yet largely unexpressed impulse that would seek to challenge the limits of pragmatism. For clinical practice to reflect a genuine concern for the alterity of the patient, a primary commitment to the analysand's individuality must be posited over, and perhaps even sometimes against, the notion of cure. One of the most basic claims made by two-person models of practice is that the therapist's clinical stance is unavoidably an expression of their own subjectivity. Ghent (1989) speaks of "the inevitability that every analyst theorizes, indeed thinks and practices on the basis of a belief system" (p. 169). If this observation is heeded with the seriousness that it warrants, then the clinical paradigm itself must also come to be questioned. A pluralistically sensitive psychoanalytic treatment cannot be justified with recourse to clinical norms.[9] If practice is to serve the creative autonomy of the analysand, we cannot rely on a preconceived goal for treatment – whether this goal is established by the analyst or patient is beside the point. The clinician's finalistic attitude has to be surrendered with the establishment of a working relationship, just as the analysand's reasons for attending treatment start to become less defined. While the patient may seek analysis for quite specific reasons and the analyst may have clear ideas about what the treatment's aims are, these justifications are necessarily sacrificed to the evolving nature of the relationship. The analysand may continue to have some sense of why they attend treatment, and the analyst may still maintain ideas as to the direction in which he or she hopes to see things progress, yet such rationalizations fail to grasp the analytic situation in its fullness. Questioning these notions clearly reflects a central aspect of the work itself.

2

RETHINKING THE PSYCHOANALYTIC SUBJECT

In the late nineteenth century, the French neurologist Hippolyte Bernheim pointedly questioned Charcot's apparent success in working with hysterical patients. The substance of Bernheim's criticism was that in the appearance of having been cured, Charcot's patients were in fact doing nothing more than hysterically complying with Charcot's own preconceptions about hysteria. Bernheim, who was himself much influenced by the practice of hypnotism, asserted that human psychology is profoundly suggestible – perhaps so much so as to render the disinterested examination of another person's mental life impossible. This claim posed a major threat to hopes that the emerging discipline of psychology might be established along properly scientific lines. As Makari (2008) explains, if everyone was subject to suggestion and blind belief: "who could be an impartial observer or an uninfluenced subject? In Bernheim's view, observer and observed, suggester and suggested, scientist and hysteric, ultimately subject and object, were impossible to distinguish with any clarity" (p. 31). Freud responded to this challenge by asking what it is that makes a person vulnerable to suggestion in the first place; he posited that suggestibility was a product of the particular features of a patient's inner world as manifested in relationship to the physician. In this way he argues for a one-person model of the psyche so as to avert the catastrophe for a scientific psychology otherwise implied.

Where might we stand today on Bernheim's outlook and the challenge it mounts to the question of personal autonomy? Thomas Nagel (1986) strikingly refers to the self as "the ultimate private object" (p. 32). Emphasizing the social nature of consciousness and in keeping with the claims of postmodernism, much recent psychoanalytic theorizing has seemingly been concerned to challenge the legitimacy of such a notion. However, if contemporary psychodynamic thinking is to remain faithful to the conventional therapeutic situation, clinicians must surely withhold from positing a notion of boundless suggestibility comparable to that claimed by Bernheim. In so far as therapy is conceived as an ethically viable service offered by one person to another, some credence has to be given to the notion of the individual. Challengingly, this idea has come to be portrayed by a wide spectrum of discourses as fundamentally antiquated. In this light, psychoanalytic thinking is placed in the distinctly awkward position of attempting to accommodate this widespread criticism without implicitly endorsing a theoretical stance that delegitimizes clinical practice.

In the previous chapter it was suggested that the extent to which psychoanalytic authority has come to be questioned demands that the field more explicitly distance itself from the medical model and its attendant notions of pathology, cure, and symptom remission. It was argued that the epistemological shift of the last thirty years would be better served by placing a greater degree of emphasis on the analyst seeking to pursue what is most particular about the analysand's experience. With this in view, it seems necessary that the notion of the subject be examined in relationship to the question of alterity. The idea of the self's fundamental "privacy" surely indicates the conceptual value still attending this notion as a means to helping the analyst remain cognizant of the ineffability of the other person. However, since relational thinking has tended to de-emphasize the role of innate endowment in favor of relational context, the notion of the private self has inevitably been minimized.

Approaching the subject

> A neutral description of the crisis of the subject as a factual occurrence is not only nonmoral [...] it is rather amoral, for it raises that which is to the measure of that which should be. In this sense, it seems to me, philosophy must always opt for the nonexistent; it must engage itself contrafactually; it must defy reality while recognizing it.
>
> (Frank, 1989, p. 10)

Historian of ideas Jerrold Seigel (2005) argues that since Descartes, theories of the self in the Western tradition have been construed along three lines: the bodily, the relational, and the reflective. An emphasis on the body tends to manifest in an image of selfhood considered to be universally valid, while the relational dimension tends to emphasize the nature of selfhood as dependent on context. Reflective notions of the self, meanwhile, have the distinctive feature of supporting some question of autonomy (whether innately given, or acquired through experience). Different theories of the self rely to varying extents on the three dimensions identified. For Seigel, the reflective aspect of selfhood must be recognized if we are to negotiate between the claims of the other two domains; achieving some reflective distance from the bodily and social is essential if a person is to mediate between their respective determinations. Nor does Seigel feel that the reflective dimension of the self can be subordinated to either the bodily (biological reductionism) or the relational (poststructuralism), since the notions of the bodily and the relational are themselves given in reflection – if these expressions are to be accepted as meaningful, then they must necessarily be considered in some respect free of the determination that they both seem to imply. David Bohm (1980) makes a similar point:

> Consider, for example, an attempt to assert that all of man's actions are con-
> ditioned and mechanical. Typically, such a view has taken one of two forms:
> either it is said that man is basically a product of his hereditary constitution,
> or else that he is determined entirely by environmental factors. However, one
> could ask of the man who believed in hereditary determination whether his
> own statement asserting this belief was nothing but the product of his heredity.
> In other words, is he compelled by his genetic structure to make such an
> utterance? Similarly, one may ask of the man who believes in environmental
> determination, whether the assertion of such a belief is nothing but the spouting
> forth of words in patterns to which he was conditioned by his environment.
> Evidently, in both cases (as well as in the case of one who asserted that man is
> completely conditioned by heredity plus environment) the answer would have
> to be in the negative, for otherwise the speakers would be denying the very
> possibility that what they said could have meaning. Indeed, it is necessarily
> implied, in any statement, that the speaker is capable of talking from intelligent
> perception, which is in turn capable of a truth that is not merely the result of a
> mechanism based on meaning or skills acquired in the past. So we see that no one
> can avoid implying, by his mode of communication, that he accepts at least the
> possibility of that free, unconditioned perception that we have called intelligence.
> (pp. 65–66)[1]

The capacity to reflect as conventionally expressed in the idea that psychoanalysis is an "insight-oriented" therapy can, in the contemporary intellectual climate, seem rather quaint. Rejecting or dramatically minimizing this notion, however, is in Seigel's view indicative of a dangerously lopsided account of selfhood. Interestingly, Seigel considers Freud's approach to be particularly notable in its flexibility and capacity to incorporate all three of the dimensions posited. Seigel's professed appreciation for Freud may surprise – the emergence of psychoanalysis is in fact often considered an intellectual milestone precisely in the destabilizing of the subject. Furthermore, Freud's thinking in respect of this notion is often unclear, particularly concerning the question of agency (Moran, 1993). Nevertheless, the *practice* of psychoanalysis appears fundamentally indicative of a commitment to the individual and of the possibility of achieving at least some degree of mastery over fate. In exploring the philosophical origins of the notion of the unconscious, Ffytche (2011) argues that this foundational idea is intimately linked with: "establishing the possibility of a self-caused self, or a self the logic of whose development is irreducibly detached from more systematic forms of explanation, or from the idea of its manipulation by external authorities or other determining causes" (p. 23). For Ffytche, Freud's de-centering of the self was announced in the context of German romanticism with the specific intention of preserving the individual's autonomy.

Since Freud's work points to the possibility of establishing an empirical basis for the philosophical unconscious, his thinking also offers significant support in the refutation of Descartes's identification of the self with the conscious mind. Just as the notion of "the soul" understood as an object of religious doctrine seemed in danger of being rendered obsolete, Freud asserts that the everyday experience of human relationships, whether in cases of overt pathology or otherwise, demonstrates that "the psyche" is nevertheless a living reality which extends beyond a person's immediate sense of themselves.[2] Nor does Freud, despite his background in neurology, seek to explain the mystery of personhood by relating the unaccounted for aspects of self directly to biology. Rather, we must contend with the intermediary of fantasy – a necessary rupture exists between the instinctual realm postulated as an object of biology, and the language of drive which is an expression of our immediate experience.

The relatively introspective nature of Freudian drive theory is apparent in that the notion of repressed drives places the accent on the subject's relationship to their own desire, while more recent psychoanalytic thinking emphasizes our relationships with others. Nevertheless, that Freud perceives the drives as being correctly directed towards the outside world rather than potentially invested in the interior life of the subject suggests that his psychology can hardly be considered introverted. Thus, a possible limitation in the relational criticism of drive theory is that in taking Freud's model as paradigmatic, the conversation is slanted from the outset towards exteriority. Although drive psychology tends towards a one-person perspective focusing on the individual, Freud's particular approach to drive is nevertheless fundamentally directed towards the environment. This tendency is also apparent in Lacanian thinking. While in stressing the subject's basic isolation from others Lacan's attitude would appear to reflect an obvious challenge to the relational outlook (most evident in terms of technique), the Lacanian approach nevertheless promotes an underlying view of the subject that is explicitly social in nature. Thus the extent to which the work of both Freud and Lacan actually offers a clear challenge to relational thinking is not as whole-hearted as it might be.

For Freud, a person becomes a problem for themselves when their way of being in the world is frustrated as a consequence of the conflictual conditions of their own subjectivity. This outlook establishes a nuanced and potentially unstable ground from which to conceptualize the individual. By associating the drives so closely with an image of the body Freud's psychology appears to focus on the private person, yet his approach to narcissism indicates that the individual's development is always to be understood in terms of their capacity to relate to their material environment. Further complicating matters, however, despite Freud's theoretical aversion to inwardness, the very notion of a psychoanalytic cure rests upon a belief in the value of insight and the possibility of achieving it. It might be argued that in Freud's thinking the principle of reason substitutes for a more adequate conception of the inner world. Furthermore, Freud's aversion to exploring this notion of interiority can be understood as having precipitated, at least on a theoretical level, several of the breaks with his major collaborators. Adler, for example, sought to question the mechanistic reductivism of Freud's approach, and his theoretical emphasis on inferiority stresses the purposiveness of individual psychology. In Jung's (1912/1916) *Psychology of the Unconscious* (the publication that precipitated his own break with Freud), Jung seeks to argue that the introversion of the libido reflected in the notion of secondary narcissism is both purposive and creative. Jung's mature work would go on to explore the nature of selfhood as articulated in the life-long task of individuation – the process of "becoming one's own self" (Jung, 1928, para. 266). It might also be noted that while Otto Rank's excommunication perhaps had more to do with the political maneuvering of other members of Freud's circle than with the theoretical content of his book on birth trauma, his break with Freud led to the development of an approach to therapy that sought to represent the creative interests of the individual over the claims of society.

In North American psychoanalysis, it was only with the emergence of Kohut's mature work that the role of teleology and the idea of the self started to gain significant mainstream attention. Kohut (1977) posits that the individual is born with certain innate qualities which, if they are to flourish, require an adequately responsive emphatic environment. He writes:

> At the moment when the mother sees her baby for the first time and is also in contact with him (through tactile, olfactory, and proprioceptive channels as she feeds, carries, bathes him), a process that lays down a person's self has its virtual beginning – it continues throughout childhood and to a lesser extent later in life. I have in mind the specific interactions of the child with his self-objects through which, in countless repetitions, the self-objects empathically respond to certain potentialities of the child (aspects of the grandiose self he exhibits, aspects of the idealized image he admires, different innate talents he employs to mediate creatively between ambitions and ideals), but not to others. This is the most important way by which the child's innate potentialities are selectively nourished or thwarted.
>
> (p. 100)

On the other side of the Atlantic, a similar outlook was voiced by Winnicott (1960) with his notion of the true self. Winnicott conceives of the individual's development as being dependent upon the interaction of "maturational processes" with the "facilitating environment" – the former can be considered commensurate with innate predisposition, while the latter constitutes the conditions upon which this endowment's realization depends. The good-enough provisions of the social environment enable the spontaneous emergence of the true self, while a failure in this respect leads to the development of a false self engendered by the need to please caregivers. Winnicott (1963a) writes:

> At the beginning the infant is entirely dependent on the physical provisions of the live mother and her womb or her infant care. But in terms of psychology we have to say that the infant is at one and the same time dependent and

independent. It is this paradox that we need to examine. There is all that is inherited, including the maturational processes, and perhaps pathologically inherited trends, and these have a reality of their own, and no one can alter these; at the same time, the maturational processes depend for their evolution on the environmental provisions. We can say that the facilitating environment makes possible the steady progress of the maturational processes.

(pp. 84–85)

Like Kohut, Winnicott argues that although human beings are undoubtedly social creatures, they are also in a fundamental sense self-contained. For Winnicott (1963b), as with Kohut, there is an essential core of the person that is partly unknowable and seemingly given from the outset: "At the centre of each person is an incommunicado element, and this is sacred and most worthy of preservation" (p. 187). Both figures consider the self to be unknowable in its essential nature and to unfold according to a pre-given plan that depends upon the environment (good-enough mothering/emphatic responsiveness) for its realization. Perhaps owing to a combination of intuitive appeal and conceptual accessibility, this kind of thinking has proven consistently attractive to clinicians. Nevertheless, the notion that the self can be considered as a secret thing that in some sense pre-exists its eventual emergence is liable to be looked upon with skepticism in the contemporary intellectual climate.

A very different perspective on selfhood was offered earlier in the twentieth century by Harry Stack Sullivan. In stark contrast to the intuitive appeal exhibited by theories of the "true" self, Sullivan's work has played a central role in prompting therapists to question their basic assumptions. For Sullivan, the self exists *only* as a construct, so that the stripping away of false representations would theoretically entail the complete dissolution of selfhood. Sullivan's view that a person consists of nothing more than the imprint of how others have perceived them connects his work with the assumptions of systems thinking. In speaking of the individual he uses the term *nexus*, which he refers back to its original sense meaning "knot" (Sullivan, 1950, p. 202). This emphasizes his contention that the subject can be understood as a social entanglement. Like Sullivan, systems theorist Gregory Bateson (1987) regards recent modes of perception as faulty and claims that attributing psychopathology to individuals is mistaken. Bateson, whose double-bind theory was a major influence on both R.D. Laing and the early development of family systems thinking, argues that mental illness is a fundamentally social phenomenon that can only be rightly interpreted in terms of systems of relationship. This apparently liberating perspective is, however, not without cost. As Rollo May (1958b) observes: "It is well known that Sullivan argued against the concept of the individual personality [yet this] opens the way to the tendency which is directly opposed to the goals of Sullivan and other interpersonal thinkers, namely, social conformity" (p. 64). Early systems theorist Ludwig von Bertalanffy (1968) foresaw a similar danger attendant to the development of the field he helped found, and warns strikingly that the emergence of systems thinking is a profoundly ambiguous event:

Man in the Big System is to be – and to a large extent has become – a moron, button-pusher or learned idiot, that is, highly trained in some narrow specialization but otherwise a mere part of the machine. This conforms to a well-known systems principle, that of progressive mechanization—the individual becoming ever-more a cogwheel dominated by a few privileged leaders, mediocrities and mystifiers who pursue their private interests under a smokescreen of ideologies.

(p. 10)

Recognizing the totalitarian connotations that can attend systems approaches, Bertalanffy stresses the importance with which the individual should be invested so as to counteract the less desirable consequences of the system. This position might also be understood to constitute a significant warning for relational theories of the unconscious. Focusing on the notion of stimulus response, Rapaport (1957) offers an early observation of the significance that the drives carry as a conceptual basis from which to establish the subject's autonomy from the environment. On a related note, Hoffman (1998) suggests that the fact that the Freudian Id is posited to be in conflict with itself precludes the possibility of a utopian politics. He contrasts this position with figures like Winnicott, Kohut, and Loewald, for whom more unified conceptions of selfhood imply the possibility of a cosmically given guiding principle (pp. 7–8). Likewise, Žižek (2009) states: "the aspiration to abolish [drive antagonism] is precisely the source of totalitarian temptation: the greatest mass murders and holocausts have always been perpetrated in the name of man as harmonious being, of a New Man without antagonistic tension" (p. xxviii).

While a conception of the self exhibiting too much unification can culminate in potentially totalitarian implications, this same danger is apparent where the conceptualization of selfhood is relativized to the brink of being spoken away completely. In contrast to Freud, whose notion of pleasure satisfaction is inherently conflictual, Sullivan sees conflict arising only as a consequence of the ways in which the needs of the child caused anxiety in caregivers. Sullivan contends that were it not for this question of the caregiver's anxiety, pleasure-seeking behaviors would be entirely integrative in nature and would tend only towards drawing people together. Thus, in a certain sense Sullivan's theory of no-self shares with Winnicottian and Kohutian notions of true self a tendency to portray human nature as existing ideally in an Edenic unspoiled state which comes to be corrupted in the pathological failures of social interaction. What this seems to indicate is that any theory of selfhood that refuses to locate a fundamental conflict within the individual *prior* to any question of interaction with the wider social environment must reckon with politically dubious implications. Furthermore, these implications can only be expected to manifest in authoritarian tendencies arising within the clinical situation – this is potentially reflected both in the maternalism of Kohutian empathy/Winnicottian holding, and in the paternalism of Sullivan's detailed inquiry.[3]

Self or selves?

For Sullivan's psychology to be clinically applicable it is necessary that he recognize the conceptual legitimacy of what he terms the "self-system," for without such a notion there appears to be no basis for treatment. It remains questionable, however, to what extent Sullivan's approach provides a basis for practice that is not fundamentally normative. Donnel Stern (1997) in fact argues that Sullivan went too far in minimizing the notion of interiority. He observes: "In a world we could not back away from, there would be no such thing as subjectivity" (p. 7). Conceptualizing the individual as a system of interpersonally constelled self-perceptions, Sullivan's work has been widely influential in offering a basis from which to challenge the idea of a unified subject. This outlook has been influential in giving rise to the popular and clinically useful notion of "self-states" (Ogden, 1977; Mitchell, 1993; Davies, 1996; Harris, 1996; Bromberg, 1998), by means of which the mind is portrayed as discontinuous and perpetually shifting between variously organized states of consciousness. This approach offers a de-centered portrayal of the self as inherently pluralistic. However, since the basis for clinical work with these states is founded in the contention that we can speak from introspective experience of their existence and hence develop a more adaptive sense of our own multiplicity, it becomes necessary to explain how a recognition of this kind might be achieved – hence, the question of insight remains. For this reason, relational theorists do not argue against the importance of achieving an overarching sense of unitary subjectivity, yet this more conventional outlook to selfhood tends to be rhetorically undermined in favor of foregrounding the notion of multiplicity. Bromberg (1998) argues for what appears to be a balanced approach honoring the extent to which self-states can be considered both as separate and connected, yet he insists that we treat the question of a unitary self as a "developmentally adaptive illusion" (p. 272). Bromberg therefore seems to privilege the isolated self-state as being in some respect more "real" than the more encompassing sense of selfhood. Thus, in an effort to challenge the theoretical emphasis on isolate individuals, Bromberg's approach comes to emphasize isolate configurations of self.

Self-states are portrayed as fundamentally relational in nature, and can be understood as an interpersonally acquired building block upon which the overarching sense of personhood is illusorily founded. In this connection, Bromberg cites Sullivan: "for all I know every human being has as many personalities as he has interpersonal relations" (Sullivan, 1950, p. 221). Emphasis in Bromberg's work is placed on the fashion in which self-states emerge in relational context, while an intrapsychic context constellating the relationship between different states only seems to be imputed in so far as it results from interpersonal negotiation – that is, the structuration of subjectivity is portrayed as being engendered by the excitation in interpersonal relationship of discrete self-states. Owing to Bromberg's emphasis on dissociation in the clinical setting, it remains unclear to what extent his notion of "standing in the spaces" might entail the idea that different aspects of self are able to dialogue creatively without prompting from an interpersonal context. Clearly the contemporary emphasis placed on the self being forged in relationship to others naturally minimizes the sense in which subjectivity is understood to be meaningfully impacted by solitude. In this light, we might wonder whether a person engaged in the act of reading a book, writing a poem, drawing a picture, playing a musical instrument, or simply day-dreaming, can be thought to carry out an activity with potential meaning for their future sense of self. Should the assumption be that they can, then the question of intrapsychic autonomy implied obviously has significant implications for clinical work. For example, Ogden (1997) argues against the conventional analytic injunction that the analysand should be encouraged to say whatever comes to mind, suggesting that an expectation of this kind is potentially disruptive in establishing a private sense of reverie. An approach of this kind reminds us that the conversation with oneself is creatively fruitful, and that it can even be disturbed through interpersonal engagement.

Like Bromberg, Mitchell (1993) claims that the sense of being a unified self is illusionary – he compares the self's apparent unity with the moving image projected from a film strip so that the appearance of continuity is engendered over time while in truth there exists only a succession of discrete self-states. However, while insisting upon the unreality of a unified sense of selfhood, Mitchell nevertheless concedes that "in some obvious way, we are the same person" (p. 106). Given Mitchell's particular take on constructivism, this appears to be an oblique reference to the body. Although Mitchell (2000) argues that we should not confuse our minds with the unity of our bodies, elsewhere he states: "constructivism will always have to be reanchored to the body and human biology to keep it grounded and emotionally relevant" (Mitchell, 1997, p. 244). He argues for the human body as a positive fact while tending to relativize any claims made about this fact as context dependent. Mitchell observes that while Freud portrayed the drives as signifying the core of the person, for more recent Freudian authors such as Kernberg and Loewald, the drives are conceived as relationally constituted. On this basis he reasons that the body cannot be regarded as the ground of our experience since our attempts to speak of it are socially constructed. However, in the distinction thus made between the unified body as an objective fact and its attributes as relational constructs, the position taken may inadvertently serve only to underscore an underlying commitment to materialism and an objective ontology. Mitchell's thinking appears to require this awkward commitment to the factual status of the body partly because any theory of subjectivity that would seek to disclaim a unitary basis for the self must account not only for the ways in which a person tends to experience his or her self as such, but also for why people in the world experience *each other* on these terms. While in the contemporary intellectual climate Mitchell and Bromberg might cogently claim that the individual's introspective sense of being a unified self is ultimately an illusion, the "obvious" sense in which we remain the same person has still to be explained. The natural fashion in which this problem is resolved from a *secular* perspective is in terms of the body – thus the singular fact of the body comes to serve as a container for the various self-states posited to engender the illusion of a coherent self.

In much the same fashion, Benjamin (1995) explicitly acknowledges the psychoanalytic necessity of retaining "the notion of the subject as a self," but then states, perhaps confusingly, that even if the self is not unitary we must continue to imagine it as such. What might be intended by "imagining" in this particular context remains unclear, and is perhaps undermined when Benjamin subsequently refers to "a being separately embodied, and in that sense an individual psyche" (p. 13). If a unitary conception of selfhood is recognized to be necessary for psychoanalytic practice and yet is only justifiable in terms of the human body, this raises significant theoretical problems. Under the circumstances, Benjamin's concern for intersubjectivity as the emergence of mutual recognition appears questionable, since the subject's imagined unity now seems to depend on the person being regarded *as an object*. In having so much minimized the notion of a unified self, Mitchell and Benjamin are forced to fall back on the idea of the body as an object to explain the self's disclosed unity to others. Despite Mitchell's emphasis on developing a psychoanalytic theory that stresses the context-dependent nature of our truth claims, in attempting to ground his approach he nevertheless finds himself relying on a stripped-down notion of the body conceived as a material fact. While seeking to promote diversity, this approach ultimately depends upon anchoring itself in an image of unity which it posits as the one objective truth. In so doing, any other image of personal wholeness – such as reflected in conceptions of the soul or spirit – is implicitly dismissed as illusion, or at best "merely" subjective.

Mitchell (1993) states: "Traditionalists and phenomenologists share the assumption that there is a stream of conscious experience that actually exists in a pristine form, to which either analyst or analysand has unmediated access, like the viewer of a film on an interior screen" (p. 60). He then critiques this notion by referencing Daniel Dennett's idea of the Cartesian theatre,[4] yet later in the same text adopts the film-strip metaphor mentioned previously (the idea of discrete self-states occurring over time creating a sense of unity) and claims that the illusion thus engendered is a meaningful one (p. 115). This is a perhaps contradictory line of argument. The value that Mitchell wishes to maintain where he states that a dismissive attitude to the illusion of a unitary self would be too literal-minded is certainly promising, yet the meaning imputed to this illusion has already been rendered trivial as a consequence of the broader tone of Mitchell's argument – this is reflected most obviously in the very use of the term "illusion." It is not sufficient merely to label something "meaningful" if everything about the theory being outlined seems to suggest otherwise. Either the self is merely an adaptive necessity, or it is valuable for its own sake. Should the former view be endorsed, then clinical work becomes nothing more than a program of brain-wiring intended to produce functional participants in the system. Given the nature of clinical practice, Mitchell is inevitably required to support the value of promoting a unified sense of selfhood, yet the emphasis of his thinking clearly favors the "truth" of the self's pluralism over the "illusion" of its unity. In so far as this emphasis is expressive of a broader rhetorical trend within the relational literature, it obscures the extent to which clinical practice must surely rely on an approach to subjectivity that to some extent runs contrary to postmodern thinking.

Autonomy and meaning

> We determine our worlds just as our worlds determine who we are. Agency remains a vital part of this dialectical process of becoming that defines us as human beings. We are always more than our contexts. There is inevitably a surfeit of meaning that cannot be reduced to the contexts or constructs we use to explain individual experience.
>
> (Frie & Reis, 2005, p. 29)

If it is necessary that we maintain some notion of organized subjectivity for clinical practice to remain theoretically justified, then the themes of autonomy and agency are also central. Where our theoretical assumptions deny the possibility of the analysand's autonomy (or, for that matter, the clinician's), this would appear to jeopardize the ethical justification for practice. As Frie (2003) observes, in the absence of an agent the therapeutic process appears meaningless. In seeming recognition of these challenges, Mitchell (1997) argues that the notion of multiple self-states needn't mean surrendering a distinction between: "self-organizations that are shallow and conformistic and self-organizations that have a long history and reflect deep affective commitments" (p. 23). This may be, yet under Mitchell's scheme of thinking it remains to be explained why the latter should be preferred over the former. Despite his interest in minimizing the reality of the unified subject, Mitchell still claims to endorse the idea of autonomy by enfolding this question within the rhetoric of meaningful illusion. Whether this approach can really be considered tenable is open to question. It seems an ethically necessary assumption that clinical practice would seek to help the analysand choose. To translate this intention to that of seeking to help the analysand attain the *illusion* of being able to choose hardly seems satisfying, yet Bromberg (1998) and Mitchell (1993) both claim that we can only attain the *sense* of agency in relationship to others. Similarly, Stolorow and Atwood (1992) argue that to speak of a person attaining agency is to attribute a subjective experience to objective reality.

Taking a more cautious approach, Aron (1996) argues that relational theory recognizes the autonomy of the individual by understanding this notion in terms of a development occurring in object relations (pp. 186–187). This position is a good deal more compatible with the ethical needs of clinical practice, yet it might be argued that locating autonomy within the context of object relations only indicates the extent to which the social matrix is being privileged as determinative. In the same text, Aron responds to Winnicott's assertion that the individual can be considered in an important sense unknown and unreachable, by interpreting this tendency as expressive of the wish to "hide" and "protect" oneself from the other (p. 234). Aron conceptualizes the question as one of revealing and concealing, thus de-emphasizing self-assertion. Object relations do indeed seem to play an important role in allowing individuals to assume some measure of control over their lives, but it might be noted that the intractability of symptomatic experience could itself be interpreted as signifying some question of the analysand's nascent autonomy. In the case of pathological suffering, the individual's autonomous functions might be understood as working to frustrate the very self arising in their stewardship. The threat that emerges in conceiving of autonomy as a developmental achievement is the same as occurs in respect to conceptions of the "true self" – a resultant danger of infantilizing the patient. Nevertheless, the question of developmental achievement Aron refers to cannot afford to be overlooked, for it points to the critical question of the patient's vulnerability.

While the theme of autonomy has become a more pressing concern with the relational emphasis on social determination, the related problem of agency has always been a feature of psychoanalytic theorizing. Moran (1993) observes that Freud tends to impute agency to the psychic apparatus so that the notion of agency is often by implication severed from the conscious subject. Nevertheless, Freud's clinical outlook is centrally concerned with helping the analysand to achieve some measure of self-mastery. Freud (1923a) states unambiguously that the goal of treatment is: "to give the analysand's ego freedom to choose one way or the other" (p. 50). This approach reflects a fundamental commitment to the Kantian notion that autonomy is established in reason (Tauber, 2009), yet Freud is also at pains to maintain an outlook compatible with the scientific standards of his day, and as such tends to avoid exploring the role of teleology. Kant, by contrast, observes that rudimentary teleological judgments appear unavoidable. Understanding what we intend by a given thing requires that we have some comprehension of its apparent purpose. Furthermore, from the requirement that we impute certain rudimentary teleological purposes to the world around us, the apparent need for a more comprehensive teleology follows – the imputing of a purpose requires clarification by way of further purposes so that this question must ultimately be asked of the world itself. In the *Critique of Practical Reason*, Kant argues that the activity of reason seeks the culmination of its own inferences in three speculative propositions which, in distinction to the pure concepts of the understanding reflected in the categories, are not directly concerned with the necessary conditions pertaining to our experience of the world itself. These propositions are the freedom of the will, the immortality of the soul, and God. They are argued not to arise from experience, but only in our efforts to unify it. Kant proposes that although the activity of reason repeatedly brings us to these ideas, their transcendent status means that they cannot be proven *or* disproven. Judgments of this kind are considered fundamentally reflective in nature, for they are not given necessarily with experience but require that experience be invested with them.

Although Freud was averse to making apparently speculative "as if" judgments of this kind, his psychology is not without teleological content – in the extent to which Freud embraces a psychological outlook, he implicitly embraces teleology. Home (2000) observes that the notions of sublimation, identification, and secondary narcissism all have a teleological bent; while Loewald (2000) perceives that a goal-oriented tendency is also clearly apparent in Freud's notion of the life instinct (p. 141). Nevertheless, Freud's opposition to teleology was a common theoretical factor contributing to his breaks with Adler, Jung, and Rank. That Freud remained unwilling to more substantially engage with the role of teleology appears indicative of his failure to more wholeheartedly depart from a biological model of mind. Husserl refers to teleology as "the form of all the forms in which subjectivity exists" (cited in Mensch, 1988, p. 307), while Jung (1952) speaks of teleology being "characteristic of everything psychic" (p. xxiii). In his late work, Winnicott (1971) builds on his ideas about transitional phenomena to develop a teleological concept of the self founded in play and the search for meaning. A commitment of this kind to the autopoietic nature of conscious life remains difficult to support within academic confines. The sensibilities of clinical psychology place a powerful expectation on psychoanalytic theorizing that it should commit to the grounding determinations of material conditions.

Where mid-twentieth-century psychoanalysis in America sought to maintain its authority by way of medicine's association with biology, the relational movement has often emphasized a commitment to the social that has resulted in numerous clinical insights and a crucial recognition of the problems attendant to positivism. However, these gains cannot afford to be at cost to a more thoroughgoing commitment to subjectivity and self-reflection. The notion of the reflective subject is seriously jeopardized in positing relationships as primary in the determination of the individual – perhaps so much so as to suggest a theoretical basis that is ethically unsupportable for the needs of a pluralistically nuanced clinical practice. Furthermore, the inevitable consequence of minimizing the role of the reflective self is that relational thinking finds itself falling back on biology wherever the claims of the social appear either inadequate or overbearing.

Getting back

> For, unless I am greatly mistaken, it is just this confrontation of object and subject, their mingling and identification, the resultant insight into the mysterious unity of Ego and actuality, destiny and character, doing and happening, and thus into the mystery of reality as an operation of the psyche – it is just this confrontation that is the alpha and omega of all psychoanalytic knowledge.
>
> (Mann, 1937, pp. 4–5)

The reductive treatment of the subject has also been significantly reflected in recent psychoanalytic efforts to theoretically overcome the Cartesian split between mind and matter. Mills (2012) contends that the subject–object divide constitutes the basis for the most controversial debate between relational schools and earlier analytic approaches (p. 37). Much relational and intersubjective thinking has indeed sought to question what Stolorow and Atwood (1992) refer to as the Cartesian "myth of the isolated mind." While efforts to overcome the split are sometimes portrayed within the psychoanalytic literature as a profoundly contemporary concern, the problem itself has a long-standing philosophical history. In so far as a position taken in this debate would seek to preserve the ontological status of the subject, there is a tendency for this issue to exhibit a distinctly romantic sensibility reflected in the endeavor to overcome disenchantment – questioning the assumptions of Cartesianism has been a central concern both of transpersonal psychology, where the dissolution of personal boundaries is associated with religious/spiritual experience, and of radical ecology, where many theorists posit that our present environmental challenges will only be adequately addressed when individuals are able to repair their presumed sense of isolation from the world.

Whether in psychoanalytic, transpersonal, or ecological context, there is a distinct tendency to portray the split as something almost pathological. Rollo May (1958b) typifies this tendency where he writes: "What is required is an approach to the world which undercuts the 'cancer,' namely, the traditional subject-object dichotomy" (p. 56). This rather aggressive take on the perceived problem is by no means unusual. Stolorow (2011) likewise refers to the "Cartesian madness" of separating thought from life (p. 102). It seems that in seeking to dissolve the myth of the isolated person, a pressing need is expressed to recover a lost image of wholeness. This is reflected in Orange's (1992) one-world epistemology of perspectival realism, and in Atwood and Stolorow (2014) going so far as to refer to the existence of disciplinary boundaries as a "tragedy" (p. 143).[5]

The intellectual preoccupation with attacking the split may in fact be counter-productive – particularly where the nature of this attack is concerned with attempting to prove that the split itself doesn't in fact exist. Philosopher Timothy Morton (2007) suggests that if there were really no subject–object divide, then it wouldn't be framed so often as a problem. He claims that if the split was not in some sense real, then seeking to critique it would be equivalent to scratching an itch that isn't there with the effect of bringing it into existence. For this reason, Morton argues that in responding to "the problem" it is precisely this kind of thinking that needs to be challenged. In keeping with this position, Frie and Reis (2005) convincingly argue for the extent to which various contemporary psychoanalytic efforts to banish Cartesianism succeed only in reinforcing it.

Although undesrcored in recent psychoanalytic thinking, problematizing the split has always been a feature of psychodynamic discourse. What is most striking about more recent approaches is the emphasis on attempting to resolve the split by *conceptually* dissolving the subject into a biologically grounded notion of the social field, rather than reflecting an *experiential* commitment to reflective insight and the Socratic notion that to know nature we must first know something of our own. Fromm (1941), for example, stresses that humanity wins freedom at cost of alienation. We thus have to achieve a higher synthesis – in William Blake's language, innocence won back from experience. The more naive romantic position (often reflected in radical ecology) supposes that we need to return to a reified conception of nature, yet in so striving, reaffirms the split. By willing as individuals to reside in a condition that would effectively annul the sense of individuality, this endeavor can only be expected to undermine itself. Responding to this observation, a participatory approach actively stresses the importance of the subject while never-theless striving to recognize the person as a process. While earlier forms of participation are understood to avoid subject–object dualism owing to the notion of a pre-reflective fusion with the environment, a contemporary approach softens Cartesianism self-reflexively by preserving "a highly differentiated though permeable individuality or *participatory self* as the agent of religious knowing" (Ferrer and Sherman, 2008, p. 38, italics in original).

Focusing on experiences of liminality, Loewald (2000) conceptualizes his own thinking with respect to disenchantment in terms of a split between reality and fantasy. This attitude seems helpful in that it has the advantage of preserving the status of the subject while emphasizing the role of ambiguity. Loewald's thinking also has resonance with Jung, whose conception of the collective unconscious offers an insufficiently recognized basis from which to explore questions of intersubjectivity. The idea of a collective psyche potentially challenges the Lacanian assumption that the imaginary order is inevitably solipsistic. Such a challenge seems important if rela-tional practitioners are to have a more substantial basis from which to justify the shift away from classical technique. Lacan's practice of stringently attending to the surface play of the patient's language reflects his contention that the idea of one subject directly recognizing another is an impossibility. In the extent to which relational thinking grounds the subject in the body conceived as an object of biology, how-ever, it too must answer to similar implications. Notions of mutual recognition are surely rendered questionable if no medium is posited through which this process can be understood to take place. If the capacity to recognize another person is an accomplishment of the imagination, the meaningfulness of this accomplishment would appear to hinge on a conception of the imaginary that in some respect transcends the individual. Should the subject be conceptualized merely as an epiphenomenon of biology, then, in a sense similar to Lacan's, we are all hopelessly marooned in our own subjectivity – any question of a meeting of minds such as to reflect a psychology of subject relations must come to seem fundamentally untenable.[6]

While Freud's approach to the unconscious emphasizes the limits of conscious intent, for Jung the "discovery" of the unconscious means something more. In addition to recognizing how this event significantly undermines the pretensions of reason, Jung also draws attention to the ways in which rational consciousness and the directed nature of our thinking may have obscured other aspects of experience that might yet be reengaged. This undertaking does not entail returning to a state of lost innocence, but rather a critical attitude is to be maintained as the modern subject reengages through fantasy with unrecognized aspects of self. Jung describes what he terms the "transcendent function" – a reconciliatory activity of the psyche that arises out of the tension between conscious and unconscious positions, poten-tially leading to the emergence of a new attitude towards life. Miller (2004) has drawn parallels between this notion and other liminal concepts such as Winnicott's transitional object, Ogden's analytic third, and aspects of Freud's thinking about the mediatory nature of the ego. Engaging in the work of what Jung refers to as "active imagination" entails becoming more receptive to the otherness of our own experience. This inevitably leads to an increased receptivity both to others *in* the environment and the otherness *of* the environment.[7] As Cheetham (2004) puts it:

> Community only exists among persons, and persons can only be perceived, perhaps they can only exist, when the walls dividing the inner from the outer begin to crumble. Only when we begin to hear the voices inside can we begin to listen to the voices outside. Then the boundary between what is mine and inside, and what is Other and outside grows ambiguous and unclear. We find ourselves immersed in the *convivium*, in community.
>
> (p. 20)

The clear advantage of such an approach lies in preserving something of the status of the individual rather than in seeking to get back to a pre-Cartesian Edenic state which has been acknowledged, even by the most vociferous psychoanalytic critics of the split, to entail unsupportable claims about the subject and the extent to which this notion can, or should, be conceptually dissolved. Nevertheless, it might also be noted that Jung's commitment to the idea that a person must always establish themselves as an agent in the world before "confronting" the unconscious in the latter half of life clearly implies a conventionally masculine developmental bias. In keeping with Nancy Chodorow's (1978) observations about the manner in which a mother's care will tend to reinforce a girl's sense of sameness and a boy's sense of difference, Carol Gilligan (1982) argues that feminine patterns of identity tend to be more directly dependent on staying related – this will naturally have implications for the experience of liminality. Nevertheless, whether following masculine or feminine[8] lines of development, in keeping with the needs of clinical practice, both developmental styles retain the notion of the autonomous self as theoretically essential. While relational thinking has helped challenge reified and unwieldy conceptions of "the ego," a pressing theoretical need has emerged in articulating which elements of this notion remain valuable, and in what ways this might now be conceptualized.

Situating the psychoanalytic subject

> The subject is the unknown because it is indeterminate, because it is a mirror, because it is foreign, because it is a totality. Therefore, in the science of the West, the subject is the all-nothing – nothing exists without it, but everything excludes it. It is the fabric of all truth, but at the same time it is nothing more than "noise" and error next to the object.
>
> (Morin, 2008, p. 25)

In the recent history of psychodynamic theorizing, the extent to which contemporary theory has been willing to draw intellectual support from beyond the field of psychology is noteworthy. While the mid-twentieth-century psychoanalytic mainstream tended to conduct its business in something of an intellectual bubble, the relational shift's emphasis on dialogue has been reflected in a corresponding openness to influence. It is perhaps understandable that part of the backlash against the conservative orthodoxy has been reflected in the idea that psychoanalysis needs to revise itself in light of new thinking and/or new research. Doubtless there is much to be celebrated in this tendency. However, it may also be that there are certain basic principles for which psychodynamic practice stands, or that emerge through the experience of doing clinical work which, while perhaps not intellectually fashionable, may yet demand our concerted support. The notion of autonomous selfhood is in this respect exemplary – it seems that analytic practice cannot sustain itself without at least some rudimentary conception of a unified and partially self-determined subject, yet it is this idea that postmodern philosophy has been most centrally concerned to question.

Fairfield (2001) makes the significant observation that while the numerous recent psychoanalytic approaches to the nature of the self reflect a range of perceptions, the differences between them are in large measure a question of rhetorical emphasis rather than reflecting a substantive differing of opinion. She contends that if one were to establish a spectrum of attitudes towards the nature of the self ranging from a perfectly isolated monism to a completely dispersed pluralism, contemporary psychoanalytic conceptions would all be grouped somewhere in the middle. This appears to reflect Wachtel's (2002) playful suggestion that rather than thinking in terms of one-person versus two-person psychologies, we might more accurately speak of the distinction between one-and-a-quarter-person theories, and one-and-three-quarter-person theories. Thus, in as much as contemporary thinking has sought to incorporate postmodern challenges to the subject, in keeping with the nature of clinical practice, clinicians still retain conceptions of selfhood that are relatively conservative. It is therefore incumbent upon contemporary practitioners to draw from philosophical accounts of the subject that not only recognize its social aspects, but also seek to accommodate for the idea of creative autonomy. A failure to reflect this notion is liable to result in unbalanced conceptions of the person, so that psychoanalytic practice either becomes theoretically incoherent or else runs the risk of rendering itself merely an exercise in social conformity.

Since the Enlightenment, Western thought has been characterized by an increasing concern with epistemology. Descartes famously claimed to have proven the fact of his own selfhood by stating that the existence of an "I" was demonstrated in the phenomenon of thinking itself. Hume would later argue against this position by suggesting that the mind is merely a bundle of sense perceptions, and that the attempt to locate the self through reason is flawed in supposing that the similarity of our thoughts implies their underlying unity. Hume wished to throw out metaphysics, claiming that all genuine knowledge can be grounded in quantitative measure. Deeply influenced by this skepticism, Kant maintained that the only metaphysical concepts directly available to us have to do with the way in which our minds structure experience in terms of time and space. Kant did not wish to disclaim the existence of a wider metaphysics, but rather to argue for the fact of such laws being fundamentally unknowable; a position encapsulated in his statement of having "had to deny *knowledge*, in order to make room for *faith*" (Kant, 1787/1998,

p. 117, italics in original). In Kant's efforts to avoid relying on an intuitive metaphysics, Terry Pinkard (2002) identifies what he refers to as the "Kantian paradox" of self-legislation. This paradox is expressed where Kant contends that the subject is bound by a moral imperative which he or she is simultaneously required to will freely:

> The paradox arises from Kant's demand that, if we are to impose a principle (a maxim, the moral law) on ourselves, then presumably we must have a reason to do so; but, if there was an antecedent reason to adopt that principle, then the reason would not itself be self-imposed; yet for it to be binding on us, it had to be (or at least had to be "regarded" to be, as Kant ambiguously stated) self-imposed.
>
> (p. 59)

For Pinkard, classical German philosophy is centrally concerned with trying to resolve the metaphysical problems of the subject raised by this paradox. Placing a fundamental value on the question of freedom, the German tradition sought to problematize and reimagine subjectivity without seeking to disclaim it. While the theme of subjectivity has been central to the development of Western philosophy from Descartes through Husserl, it is in the context of the classical German tradition that this question is engaged most exhaustively. Thus, the fate of the subject in Western discourse can be thought significantly dependent on the perceptions we have of the fate of this tradition. Conventional understanding has portrayed German idealism as having been inaugurated with the problems raised by Kant in the *Critique of Pure Reason*, to subsequently proceed through a series of transitional positions reflected in the ideas of several lesser figures, only to find logical culmination in the philosophy of Hegel. According to this reading, the work of the "intervening" figures in this movement – most notably that of Jacobi, Reinhold, Fichte, and Schelling – is perceived as being of significantly less importance than that of the two major thinkers bookending them.

This particular rendering of intellectual history also happens to be reflected in the widely influential interpretation of this tradition offered by none other than Hegel himself. For this reason, a significant sense in which Hegel can be understood to have shaped contemporary attitudes towards subjectivity is in the extent to which he succeeded in establishing a reading of the contribution of his contemporaries that privileged his own work as its summation and logical completion. Hegel's broader concern for history also foregrounds the importance of this theme for metaphysical thinking, thus laying the groundwork for the contextual undermining of metaphysics that would emerge in the twentieth century – while Hegel uses history as a justification for his metaphysical project, later thinkers would increasingly come to regard history as *determinative* of philosophy rather than as the basis for its justification. In addition, the totalizing truth claims of the Hegelian system have significantly contributed to the further development of a basic skepticism towards metaphysics which has thus accelerated the conceptual dissolution of the subject. Finally, as expressed by way of the master–slave dialectic, Hegel's claims for the role of intersubjectivity extend beyond those of Fichte and

Schelling to suggest that self-consciousness is not only dependent on intersubjectivity but is *explained* by it. This position opens the way for subsequent thinkers to conclude that the self is an unnecessary metaphysical postulate, and that self-consciousness is always already formed in the context of intersubjective communication.

Subsequent to Hegel, the two figures widely considered most influential in having inaugurated the project to abandon the notion of the subject are Nietzsche and Heidegger. When Nietzsche's Zarathustra pronounces the death of God he is also effectively announcing the end of metaphysics. In *On the Genealogy of Morality*, Nietzsche subsequently argues that the notion of the subject is the primary metaphysical error. He conceives of the subject as an illusion of unity that was established out of human weakness. Human beings are understood to have functioned originally as creatures of pure instinct whose consciousness was directed towards the outside world. Only as a consequence of civilization and the constraints of living with other people is self-consciousness forced unnaturally into existence. This process is portrayed as culminating in the internalization of the law manifesting in the sense of moral agency so highly prized by Kant. Thus Nietzsche's attempt to discredit the subject is intimately bound to his challenging ethical philosophy.

While a reification of truth will always make destructive claims on the other, the absolute refusal of truth appears to result in an ethical groundlessness that seems untenable in the context of clinical practice. If the profession of psychoanalysis is to endorse basic principles of ethical conduct, then the notion of selfhood cannot afford to be skipped over with passing reference to adaptive illusion. The humanistic traits of contemporary practice[9] are reflected in a basic commitment to the value of persons, yet as Heidegger (1947/1977) unambiguously reminds us: "every humanism is either grounded in a metaphysics or is itself made to be the ground of one."

Heidegger further confirms Nietzsche's rejection of the subject. The insurmountable problems he perceives in this notion are explicitly understood to signal the exhaustion of the Western metaphysical tradition. Heidegger (1927/1962) claims that the concept of being since the time of Greek philosophy has been defined in terms of presence so as to enable access to meaning. He argues that the notion of the subject is born out of an impulse towards self-preservation and domination. In Heidegger's view, despite Nietzsche's contribution towards dispelling the idea of a unified self, his doctrine of power still reflects a metaphysical anthropocentrism. Following on the work of Nietzsche and Heidegger, Foucault (1970) claims that "human nature" was an invention of the eighteenth century, and that Nietzsche's "overcoming of man" necessarily implies the immanent "death of man." For Foucault, the subject is coerced into existence through the operations of power. He observes that the notion of the person in Western discourse suffers from a fundamental contradiction in being conceived both as an object of empirical inquiry and as a transcendental subject in which all experience can be grounded.

While the postmodern critique of the subject is associated most directly with French poststructuralism, this notion also comes under fire from within critical theory. Second generation critical theorists have voiced a widespread resistance to endorsing a return to subjectivity, preferring theories that emphasize the role of language and intersubjectivity. In their efforts to bring about social change these figures seek to question any sense of essentialism, and hence in a fashion that might seem to undermine their own agenda resist endorsing the question of individual autonomy. As Nagel (1986) puts it in reference to the broad tendency towards historicism: "in the name of liberation, these movements have offered us intellectual repression" (p. 11). Carr (1999) observes that while much Continental thinking in the last fifty years has been centrally concerned with defending the claims of the particular and local over those of the universal and absolute, this line of thinking has perversely depended upon a totalizing view of the history of philosophy offered by Heidegger wherein it is claimed that philosophy has followed an inevitable trajectory since Descartes's *cogito* culminating in the imputed failure of Husserl's phenomenology and Sartre's existentialism. Carr writes:

> One irony in this development is that Continental philosophy thus joins hands in an important respect with the heirs of positivism in the analytic tradition. Subjectivity has always been an embarrassment to those who would reduce the world to what can be understood by the natural science of the day. From Ryle's philosophical behaviorism of the 1940s to the efforts of today's neuro-logically oriented materialists, philosophers in this tradition have labored mightily to alienate subjectivity because it will not conveniently fit into the seamless materialist ontology that they accept in advance and without argument.
>
> (p. 4)

In his critique of the Heideggerian account of the history of philosophy, Carr draws attention to the fashion in which Heidegger's approach appears to deny a fundamental aspect of conventional historical narrative, this being the notion that human thought and action might play some role in shaping the events of history. For Heidegger, the history of philosophy appears to determine philosophical endeavor rather than philosophical activity determining the history of philosophy. It is important to again note that this line of thinking cannot be considered in keeping with the assumptions upon which analytic practice tends to base itself. In the context of the clinical situation, it must necessarily be granted that a person's life course can be affected in some meaningful respect by way of self-reflection and directed human action. In order to be ethically defensible, analytic practice must insist that human beings can obviate the more extreme claims of power and language. Even while analytic thinking may often be enriched in acknowledging these claims, for psychoanalysis to remain applicable as a clinical practice analysts must in some extent oppose them.

Within contemporary Continental philosophy, Jürgen Habermas is the most prominent spokesperson for the notion that the hopes of modernity have not been entirely extinguished. While supporting an effort to resuscitate the modernist project, Habermas nevertheless gives his full endorsement to the end of metaphysics and the death of the subject. As a critical theorist, however, this acceptance leaves Habermas having to provide an account of how persons are to resist manipulation by systemic power. If the notion of the subject has been delegitimized and "the paradigm of consciousness is exhausted" (Habermas, 1987, p. 296), how can the idea of progress still be supported? In order to retain a philosophical stance that maintains the possibility of the human community developing towards greater freedom, Habermas argues that self-consciousness is not merely a product of impersonal power (as Foucault claims), but rather is a product of relational exchange and the internalization of intersubjective dialogue.

Owing to his emphasis on intersubjectivity, Habermas's work is often cited in support of contemporary relational thinking. In keeping with relational and intersubjective perspectives, Habermas is significantly influenced by George Herbert Mead's theory of social interactionism. Mead (1964) claims that the self emerges primarily out of interaction with others. However, Mead also makes a distinction between what he terms the "me" and the "I." The me develops out of internalized interactions with other people, while the I is a pre-social disposition expressive of primitive needs and desires. The emergence of self-consciousness is in Mead's view dependent on being able to distinguish between these two senses of self, and thus to attain a degree of separation between the individual and the culture. For Mead, the "I" is the basis both for freedom and for the possibility of change and novelty. In contrast to this position, Habermas does away with the pre-linguistic elements of subjectivity reflected in Mead's biological emphasis and argues that the self is only a linguistic construct. However, the problem with a conception of the self that is purely intersubjective arises from the fact that, as Dews (1996) puts it: "the other's reaction as directed towards *me* already presupposes an awareness of myself. Without this, I would not be able to distinguish such reactions from those towards third parties: the object 'Me' could not even be constituted as an indifferent object among others" (p. 179). Thus, Habermas (1994, Chapter 2) has since conceded that a rudimentary awareness of self must exist prior to relationship.

What are we to make of this pre-relational self? In having come to allow for such a notion, Habermas has effectively conceded ground to Dieter Henrich, his main philosophical rival in Germany. Within the English-speaking world Henrich is a name less well known than that of Habermas. He is most recognized as a leading interpreter of the German Idealist tradition, but his work is also centrally concerned with an attempt to revive the philosophy of subjectivity – two domains of endeavor that he perceives to be intimately connected.[10] For Henrich and his followers (sometimes referred to collectively as "the Heidelberg School") the notions of intersubjectivity and agency that Habermas endorses necessitate a return to the philosophy of consciousness that he rejects.

A foundational aspect of Henrich's attempt to restore philosophical respectability to the notion of the self is constituted in his return to Fichte. Henrich (1982) asserts that Fichte's theory of self-consciousness offers a compelling position which, as a consequence of the intellectual dominance of Hegel, has not been sufficiently recognized or pursued by the Western philosophical tradition. Fichte's work draws attention to the inadequacies of any theory of self-consciousness that would seek to found itself in the notion of reflection. Approaches of this kind treat objects of the inner life just as they do those belonging to the outside world. In this way, self-consciousness is understood in terms of the self having made itself an object to itself. As Kant had already recognized, however, the attempt to define the self in this way presupposes the self, and is thus inescapably circular. Henrich (2003) explains:

> I cannot concentrate on something unless there is already some awareness of it [...] reflection can only make an awareness I already have *explicit*. Moreover, it might possibly lead to a descriptive knowledge about the self, but reflection does not account for the *original* self-awareness.
>
> (p. 255, italics in original)

This problem leads Fichte to posit a pre-reflexive notion of the self as absolute: a primordial essence constituting the condition upon which reflection occurs as a secondary phenomenon. In distinction to Fichte and expressing the influence of Schelling, Henrich's approach suggests that self-consciousness is an event that precedes the self rather than something which is generated by it. The emergence of the self is conceived as the emergence of an organizing structure in consciousness – the subjective conditions out of which the self is formed are not self-caused, but determinate upon a transcendent ground.

Henrich thus makes a distinction between the "person" understood as an individual, and the "subject" understood as the primordial self-consciousness upon which the emergence of the person depends. Encapsulating this position, Dews (1996) states: "As persons, we are in the world; as subjects we transcend it as a whole" (p. 180). For Henrich, the effort to resolve this paradoxical state of affairs is a fundamental human motivation that drives the course of history. The metaphysical project that Henrich endorses is thus animated by the effort to offer interpretations of experience that maintain an awareness of the relationship between the empirical person and the transcendent subject. Henrich's metaphysics of subjectivity seeks to stress the importance for the individual of addressing the big questions, since our selfhood is fundamentally grounded in them. Significantly, Henrich (1987a) also insists that this project need not require endorsing a rigid foundationalism:

> Revisionary metaphysics is interpretation of conscious life on the part of conscious life. It is by no means the disclosure of a supramundane realm which we could conceive as the domain into which we have to transform ourselves. What undergoes transformation is our understanding of ourselves and our condition. The very world in which we live appears in a new light once it has become subject to new description.
>
> (p. 122)

Henrich's most well-known pupil, Manfred Frank (1989), offers a compelling refutation of Heidegger's critique of the subject. Self-acquaintance is considered by Henrich and his followers to spring from primordial origins that the self cannot master nor gain direct access to. Fichte speaks of the subject's "absolute dependence" and

Schelling adopts the notion of "unprereflective Being" founded in a basis that lies beyond relationship. The notion that subjectivity is dependent upon an unconscious ground to which it is beholden appears to refute Heidegger's claim that the philosophy of subjectivity is fundamentally concerned with domination and self-preservation. For Henrich, the impulse to self-preservation indicates that self-consciousness is in some sense aware that it depends upon a ground that it cannot control. Supporting this, Frank draws attention to how the German romantics coming after Fichte tended not to conceive of subjectivity in terms of an "I." Heidegger's fundamental ontology claims that the Western tradition has come to interpret being as presence, and that the subject is posited to exist as something that presents itself to itself reflectively. Frank argues that this line of thinking – which is voiced also in the work of Foucault, Derrida, and Lacan – is only applicable to certain figures in the philosophical tradition. While Heidegger's approach can be justified in respect to thinkers like Kant, Hegel, and Husserl, it misses the mark in respect to Fichte, Schelling, the early German romantics, Brentano, and Sartre. Frank argues that all of these figures reject self-reflective theories of consciousness on the basis that the self cannot know itself through reflecting upon itself without having had a prior awareness of itself. In sum, Heidegger and his followers tend to conflate self-consciousness with self-reflection despite the fact that the limits of this approach have been known since at least the time of Fichte.

Clearly our attitude towards the history of ideas plays a decisive role in shaping the perceived viability of pursuing certain lines of thinking. The current status of the subject within Continental philosophy has been significantly shaped by the influence of those readings of history offered by Hegel and Heidegger – in the case of Hegel, by shaping the perception that the classical German philosophy of the subject should be interpreted through his own work as its logical culmination, and in Heidegger, by offering a powerful reading of all Western philosophy shown to culminate in the collapse of metaphysics in the early twentieth century. Both of these accounts are of course marked by an underlying concern for justifying the finality of the philosopher's own point of view. The closed nature of these readings has been reinforced by their widespread influence. There is surely an irony, however, in the extent to which thinking that claims to question narratives of domination has nevertheless often relied upon an oppressive approach to intellectual history that, in its very attempt to disclaim essentialism, remains implicitly wed to the idea of progress.[11] In response to this state of affairs, Henrich offers an intriguing proposition. He introduces the notion of what he refers to as a *Denkraum* or "conceptual space." Henrich (1997) writes:

> A movement in thought can never be understood in terms that lack a motivating force for thought itself, that is, in the form of reasons. When thought takes such a fruitful turn, it must have been preceded by a novel arrangement of conceptual problems and possibilities, an arrangement that had come to seem inescapable. One could say a conceptual space (*Denkraum*) opens up that provides a basic orientation for the development of particular conceptual styles

and achievements, and whose coordinate system can then be filled in by theories in definite ways.

(p. 94)

The emergence of a *Denkraum* is engendered by conditions established in the activity of thinking, and it is out of these conditions that latent possibilities for thought arise – thoughts that may not yet have been thought, and which have only been registered thinkable with the emergence of this conceptual space. Those who brought the *Denkraum* into being often do not fully grasp the possibilities for thought thus arising. Returning to a largely discarded *Denkraum* entails thinking into the unthought spaces. The *Denkraum* can be considered contextually dependent but also, in the extent to which this thought space has yet to be fully explored, still potentially vital – that is, the untapped liveliness of the unthought thoughts actually facilitates our engagement with the context-dependent elements, just as engaging deeply with the context can potentially evoke the *Denkraum*. This approach to history is enlisted in support of Henrich's project to reengage classical German philosophy in order to resuscitate those lines of thinking that he perceives as having been insufficiently realized.

Henrich and his followers thus offer a compelling theoretical basis from which to return to the intellectual milieu out of which depth psychology emerged, and they do so in support of the continued viability of a philosophy of the subject upon which contemporary psychoanalysis still depends. For Henrich, metaphysical thinking reflects the spontaneous efforts of the subject to attain a complete self-description – a project which can never finally succeed, yet is absolutely necessary if individuals are to resist the ideological impositions of false consciousness. The following chapter will consider how Henrich's attempt to argue for a non-foundationalist metaphysics might complement a participatory approach to Jung's thinking about the archetype. This approach is offered as a possible basis from which practitioners might more effectively work with their own subjectivity, thus better allowing for the alterity of the patient.

3

PLURALISM AND BELIEF

At the heart of the relational shift is a concern for the context-dependent nature of our truth claims. This recognition has destabilized clinical authority, causing practitioners to search for new ways in which to conceptualize professional expertise. While the classical model has been conventionally understood to entail long periods of communicative abstention punctuated by interpretive moments of revealed truth, relational thinking extensively challenges both the idea of analytic neutrality and the notion of a final truth that awaits the analyst's discovery. This questioning of assumptions has been necessary if psychoanalytic practice is to engage with the tasks emerging as a consequence of the challenges of cultural diversity. One response to these challenges has been expressed in the effort to abstain from making assumptions altogether. Thus, Brandchaft (2010) states: "What I see as pivotal in an emancipatory approach to psychoanalysis is the analyst's capacity to liberate his own vision of what is true or best for his analysand, let go of such preconceptions, and start anew" (p. 25). While laudable in its intent, a position of this kind is also problematic. Put simply, we can only intentionally suspend our judgements by effectively making a judgement upon judgement itself – in directly seeking to exclude judgement, we only confirm the impossibility of doing so.

In the extent to which contemporary psychoanalytic approaches have reacted against the dogmatisms of the past by disavowing speculative thinking, the danger now arising is that our most basic assumptions go unrecognized as such. Nowhere is this tendency more apparent than in approaching questions of spirituality.[1] Consider, for example, the case of a patient presenting with a belief that a particular problem is the consequence of karma carried over from a previous lifetime. If a relationally oriented practitioner is to work with this belief without implicitly passing final judgement on it, then it seems necessary that he or she relinquish their own theoretical assumptions as to the self being a fundamentally relational construct. This is easier said than done, however, when the theoretical frame by means of which this conflict comes to be apprehended is itself an expression of the problem – our capacity to recognize the conflict thus seems to depend on willing its very existence. Furthermore, with the problem now recognized as such, there can be no question of a retreat – any attempt to surrender our assumptions would entail a fruitless act of dishonesty, since the motivation for such a surrender would itself lie within the very system of belief that the practitioner seeks to abandon.

In so far as our theoretical commitments are expressions of who we are and how we understand the world, they are not merely to be switched out or suspended. The popular conceit that our beliefs are interchangeable is reflected in the oft adopted metaphor that our biases might be conceptualized as "lenses" which can effectively be removed and replaced so as to "try on" a different worldview. Robert Kegan's (1982, 1994) work illustrates the dangers of such a position. Although his approach to psychological growth suggestively contends that the object of each stage in his developmental schema is the subject of the stage that came before it, Kegan nevertheless comes to portray thirdness as characterizing a stable order of consciousness – one which he even suggests reflects the highest point of human development. In this way, an ideology is in danger of being made out of so-called "trans-ideological" thinking. To maintain a more clinically responsible attitude, we might stay closer to Kegan's fundamental insight that our biases can only be suspended to the extent that they are no longer our biases. If we are to avoid killing with kindness, perhaps the most that should be hoped for (at least initially) is some willingness to recognize (and endure) conflict with the other.

With this dynamic in mind, it is notable that while the shift from drive to relationship makes direct claims on belief, the shift towards constructivism is inclined more towards relativizing truth claims than asserting them. Nevertheless, it must be admitted that the constructivist standpoint tends to absolutize its own ideas as to the role of context while relativizing all other truth claims. Given this tendency, postmodern thinking's relationship to spirituality can be regarded as distinctly ambiguous. On the one hand, it would appear that in seeking to disrupt grand narratives postmodernism contradicts the sensibilities of formalized religion – explicitly post-metaphysical ways of thinking effectively deny religion any ontological significance beyond the play of language. On the other hand, and for much the same reason, the postmodern outlook also offers a means of questioning those aspects of the modernist project which claim to have left religious belief obsolete. Hauke (2000) suggests:

> Postmodern views offer depth psychology the chance to restore its otherness, its spiritual and religious element which was always the ground from which it sprang but which became lost through depth psychology clinging to, rather than continuing to challenge, the modernist values within which it emerged.
>
> (p. 209)

Contradicting this claim, in the early history of transpersonal psychology postmodernism tended to be perceived more as a possible threat than an asset, and the field relied heavily on the claims of the "perennial philosophy" – a grand-narrative approach to comparative religion encapsulated in the idea of one truth with many paths. Jorge Ferrer (2002) employs a participatory approach to powerfully question the overarching truth claims associated with transpersonal psychology's reliance on perennialist assumptions.

Ferrer (2008) suggests that efforts to explain conflicting religious truth claims have tended to assume one of three forms: "dogmatic exclusivists" argue that only their own system of belief reflects the final truth; "hierarchical inclusivists" likewise take their own tradition to be final, yet concede that other systems of belief may grasp religious truth incompletely; while "ecumenical pluralists" approach religious divergences with the idea that all systems of belief ultimately point to the same basic metaphysical reality. All three approaches share the objectivist assumption of a singular plane of spiritual truth, and only vary in the extent to which they grant other traditions access. In seeking to question this notion Ferrer's work draws from Varela et al.'s (1991) notion of enaction – a term which these authors adopt to express the idea that embodied action gives rise to a world of cognitive distinctions consequent upon the relationship between organisms and their environment. In this light, knowledge is not considered to depend on the representation of a pre-given reality, but rather the environment as we experience it is brought into existence in an active process that can be considered fundamentally transformative. Ferrer extends this concept to suggest that the participatory turn reflects an enactive understanding of the sacred, so that religious/spiritual experiences are to be understood as co-creative events. These participatory events are not considered to take place "inside" a mind, nor do they "happen to" an individual – rather, they are enacted in the relationship between self and world (Hartelius & Ferrer, 2013, p. 197). In breaking down the Kantian distinction between *noumena* and *phenomena* to posit that cognition is actively implicated in the world itself, this approach is argued to be epistemologically constructivist yet metaphysically realist (Ferrer and Sherman, 2008, p. 35), thus avoiding the tendency of reductively perceiving spirituality as "only" a construct of culture, while at the same time abstaining from religious or metaphysical dogmatism.

The participatory outlook is argued to offer an approach to transpersonal thinking that can accommodate a genuinely pluralistic spirituality without surrendering to the threat of relativism that naturally seems to arise as a consequence of contextualism. Rather than seek to assimilate sometimes contradictory spiritual insights into an overarching theory of everything, Ferrer shows how thinking in terms of spirituality as a participatory unfolding enables the transpersonal to be considered inherently pluralistic. From this perspective, variations in the perception of life's disclosed meaning are not to be finally reconciled with the notion of a fixed truth, but rather truth itself emerges out of its own contradictions as enacted in the diversity of human life. Thus Ferrer demonstrates how a participatory approach to spirituality can incorporate postmodern uncertainty without reductively relativizing our truth claims.

While the postmodern turn in psychoanalytic thinking coupled with the clinical need to recognize diversity has encouraged the profession to treat spirituality with more respect, engagement with this challenge remains half-hearted. In a relational text that seeks to explore the interface between psychoanalysis and spirituality, Sorenson (2004) writes:

> The goal is not to spiritualize psychoanalysis, to psychoanalyze spirituality, or to harmonize or minimize differences by subsuming one discipline into the other, but rather to let each stand in genuine conversation with the other and to welcome ongoing difference.
>
> (p. 26)

This passage is suggestive of the possible limits of contemporary psychoanalytic thinking in attempting to more adequately comprehend the challenge laid down by divergent belief systems – in this frame of reference, psychoanalysis continues to be considered as a discrete system that can somehow "encounter" spirituality. A position of this nature overlooks the extent to which different systems of psychoanalytic belief in themselves reflect different commitments of spirit. A person's spirituality is expressed out of who they are, and cannot be cordoned off as if it were merely an aspect of their personality. The outlook adopted by Sorenson is reflective of the often encountered attitude in mainstream clinical psychology that spirituality can be treated as a "domain of life" so that the clinician's fundamental worldview remains untroubled (Tennes, 2007; Brown, 2015a).[2] Theologist Marcus Pound (2007) suggests that efforts to integrate psychoanalysis with spirituality have always tended to sell theology short by assuming the autonomy of the secular sphere and treating God as something like a supplemental bonus to regular functioning – salvation thus becomes equivalent to achieving a healthy ego. In seeking to respond to this criticism, we might consider how the field may be shaped in attending to recent claims that psychoanalytic work can be conceptualized both as a form of prayer (Eigen, 1998) and as a fundamentally religious practice (Aron, 2004).

If the influence of postmodernism has provided the opportunity for psychoanalysis to engage more deeply with the question of spirituality, it would seem dependent on pursing the implications of a constructivist outlook without delimiting these claims by grounding them in a materialist paradigm. Making this commitment entails taking up a challenging theoretical point of view that is clearly out of step with commonplace assumptions, and yet this is surely necessary if we would seek to approach a patient's suffering without dictating to it. As the Western frame of reference was approaching the seeming possibility that religion could be done away with completely, in reflecting the persistent claims of the irrational as expressed in the symptomatology of patients, the challenge of psychiatry remained. This struggle is of course foremost in the work of Freud – in many respects a profoundly religious man, who was nonetheless a devout atheist. Thus, in the works and character of the figure usually portrayed as the field's founder, a tension can be discerned between the claims of Enlightenment on the one hand, and a profound recognition of the insufficiency of reason on the other. While emphasizing depth, the extent to which Freud's (1933) approach ultimately comes to reflect an attitude of overcoming is suggested when he writes: "Our best hope for the future is that intellect – the scientific spirit, reason – may in the process of time establish a dictatorship in the mental life of man" (pp. 171–172). The one-sidedness of this position no longer seems tenable, yet the need of adopting a theoretical outlook that accommodates epistemological uncertainty presents major challenges.

Aron (1996) is keenly aware of the problems that arise if psychoanalytic practice is to embrace postmodern thinking. Perhaps more pressing even than the threat posed to the analyst's claim to expertise are the implications for professional ethics. Aron states:

> I want to assert in the strongest possible terms that the abandonment of metapsychological truths and theoretical foundations does not necessitate the surrender of ethical standards, professional responsibility, or clinical judgement. [...] I believe that an acceptance of the relational-perspectivist approach that has guided my thinking throughout this book leads to the recognition that analysts must accept responsibility for the fact that it is their own personality, their own subjectivity, that underlies their values and beliefs, that infuses their theoretical convictions, and that forms the basis for their technical interventions and clinical judgement.
>
> (p. 259)

It remains to be asked, however, why analysts *must* accept the responsibility Aron speaks of. Why is the analyst to come to this particular conclusion rather than, for example, discerning that "everything is permitted" and pursuing a Nietzschean project of domination? The ethical claim Aron makes here is not postmodern, so much as unabashedly Kantian. As Manfred Frank (1995a) argues, however, such a claim demands an absolute theoretical commitment to the irreducible nature of our subjectivity:

> After all, how am I to take seriously something like Kant's categorical imperative, according to which I am to treat persons fundamentally as ends, not as objects, if persons just are objects and nothing more? If there is nothing like nonobjective subjectivity, then this imperative loses its addressee. Thus argumentation and ethics need a "fundamentum in re." In my opinion, this is the irreducibility of subjects to objects.
>
> (p. 178)

A similar problem has been raised by Nagl (1988) with respect to Habermas's inter-subjective-communicative paradigm. As Dews (1996) puts it: "we still need to be able to account for the 'ideality' of practical reason which is apparent in the subject's capacity to respond to the intersubjective validity of moral claims in abstraction from all considerations of interest" (p. 186). The dissolution of the philosophy of the subject, having reached its culmination in the work of Heidegger, finds itself on rocky ground ethically.

An early criticism of Heidegger's fundamental ontology is provided by Levinas, for whom Heidegger's emphasis on being is one-dimensional and not tenable as a final basis for philosophy. Under the influence of Levinas's philosophy of the other, Continental philosophy underwent something of an ethical turn in the late twentieth century. An encounter with the other is required by Levinas (1999) to always be grounded in the notion of the stranger; difference must not be allowed to collapse into the possible violence implied in a reduction to the same. The other is unattainable and breaks free from any context: "there is no fusion: the relation to the other is envisioned as alterity" (p. 103). For Levinas, a meeting with what he terms "the face" of the other entails an ethical responsibility. In this context, Levinas relies significantly upon a notion of transcendence. This idea of transcendence is not conceived as signifying a world into which one can pass over and escape from life, but rather as being concerned with the preservation of the other as such.[3]

Levinas (1961/1969) writes: "metaphysical desire tends toward *something else entirely*, toward the *absolutely other*" (p. 33, italics in original). This notion of metaphysical desire is linked with establishing the ground of an ethical relationship to the other; an encounter with the other which places the "I" in question, thus giving rise to transcendence. Levinas (1999) writes:

> In the naturalness of being-with-respect-to-that-being-itself, in relation to which all things – and even the other man – seem to take on meaning, essential nature is called into question. A turning on the basis of the face of the other, in which, at the very heart of the phenomenon, in its very light, a surplus of significance is signified that could be designated as glory. It demands me, requires me, summons me. Should we not call this demand or this interpellation or this summons to responsibility the word of God? Does not God come to mind precisely in that summons, rather than in the thematization of the thinkable, rather even than in some invitation to dialogue? Does not that summons to responsibility destroy the forms of generality in which my store of knowledge, my knowledge of the other man, represents the latter to me as similar to me, designating me instead in the face of the other as responsible with no possible denial, and thus, as the unique and chosen one?
>
> (p. 27)

The proximity of God experienced in this encounter requires that we give of ourselves without seeking anything in return. Something is owed to our neighbor with no expectation of reciprocity. It is in this respect that Levinas's work departs most clearly from the influence of Martin Buber. While Buber conceives of the relationship with the other as symmetrical, Levinas posits a fundamental asymmetry that is reflected in the ethical demand made upon us in an encounter with the other's face. Buber's (1937) conception of the I–Thou relationship, which significantly influenced Levinas's work, is considered by Levinas to place too much emphasis on the notion of the I reaching out in active relationship to embrace a Thou. Levinas's encounter with the face of the other calls forth a radical responsibility – a demand that the other's face makes from beyond the same, and which is conceived to be infinitely unanswerable.

In the context of the analytic situation, Levinas's philosophy is clearly thought-provoking. Orange (2009) goes so far as to affirm his work as expressing an appropriate ethic for clinical practice. To seek to follow this line of thinking, however, raises serious challenges. Tellingly, Levinas's work would appear to throw considerable suspicion on Sullivan's (1940) often endorsed statement that "we are all much more simply human than otherwise" (p. 39).[4] Sullivan seeks to understand the analysand by respecting the otherness of their language, yet the assumption seemingly remains that the underlying experience is a familiar one. By contrast, Levinas mobilizes the idea of transcendence as a way of protecting the other from the violence of the same. In a fashion that might be regarded as significant for relational thinking, Levinas (1999) perceives that Western thought successfully emancipated itself from the transcendence of the One, only to discover it again in the unity of the system (p. 11). Seeking to counteract the tendency to reify the image of material conditions as the new ground of unity, in approaching the other as such it becomes necessary to postulate a factor thought to reside beyond the system as it stands.

Questioning motives

> Unfortunately there are many people who have a wrong idea of metaphysics; they wish to exclude from human life all that they cannot grasp directly. By doing this we would limit the potential development of every new idea.
>
> (Adler, 1938, pp. 275–276)

Possibly the most striking feature of the academic discipline of psychology is the extent to which the field has effectively rejected the very standpoint with which it claims to concern itself – that is, the study of the human subject. By contrast, one of the most striking features of Freud's thinking is the degree in which his work reflects an outlook that can justifiably be characterized as psychological. This state of affairs places psychoanalytic endeavor in a peculiar relationship to the wider discipline of psychology, for it saddles psychodynamic discourse with the thankless task of upholding the very attitude that the wider field fails to reflect. Efforts to meet this responsibility are further impaired by the ways in which American psychoanalysis has been shaped institutionally. While the medicalization of psychoanalysis helped promote Freud as a "biologist of the mind" (Sulloway, 1979), the more recent relational shift has emphasized the constitutional role of social life. Thus, in contrast to Freud's emphasis on fantasy, the American psychoanalytic mainstream has consistently sought to establish a basis from which to study the mind that is not itself mental. In seeking to challenge this tendency, the concept of drive might be considered important not only as a means to balancing the relational emphasis on the social, but also in some measure as a way of refuting the conservative emphasis on the biological.

That Freud's mature work was founded in his failed project for a scientific psychology indicates that psychoanalysis has been shaped by the need to express a vision that could not be supported by the commonly accepted perception of the material facts. This is an intriguing notion that has tended to be seen as a potential embarrassment, rather than suggesting something essential about the field's emancipatory ethos. Freud's background in neurology has often been taken as a justification for the endeavor to draw from contemporary science in an effort to steer his work back towards biology. From this perspective, the psychological nature of Freud's approach can start to seem like a stop-gap measure – something of a theoretical compromise while scientific research catches up. Readings of this kind frequently draw support from claims about what Freud "would have wanted" had he been alive today. Thinking in this way ignores the tremendous value of the paradigmatic shift to a psychological model for the development of a clinical approach placing fundamental importance on the experience of the individual.

In 1915, with the publication of "Instincts and Their Vicissitudes," Freud speaks of the drives as a borderline phenomenon: "a concept on the frontier between the mental and the somatic" (Freud, 1915a, pp. 121–122). This borderline designation certainly seems apt considering the extent to which Freud vacillates between referring to the drives in psychological versus physiological terms. While Freud is sometimes said to have given up on a biological outlook when he abandoned his scientific project, the extent to which he actually departed from a body-based explanation of the drives is certainly questionable – he famously contends that "the ego is first and foremost a bodily ego" (Freud, 1923a, p. 20), and not that the body is first and foremost a construct existing in fantasy. Nevertheless, the potentially radical nature of the psychological outlook is reflected as late as 1933, where Freud states unabashedly: "The theory of the drives is, so to say, our mythology. Drives are mythical entities, magnificent in their indefiniteness" (Freud, 1933, p. 95).

Klein furthers the concept of drive with her extended notion of unconscious phantasy, but like Freud she continues to understand phantasy as a derivative of biology. Making phantasy conscious means a confrontation with material reality and, being biologically determined, it is from the field of material reality that the phantasy ultimately derives. Thus for Freud and Klein, phantasy is conceived as a necessary medium to work with, but not as intrinsically valuable in its own right. The underlying mythology informing a person's behaviors has to be uncovered so that the individual can more accurately experience the objective truth of a world that the phantasy life obscures. Owing to the association of drives with bodily satisfaction, drive gratification is regarded as inevitably self-interested. It is therefore considered both necessary and appropriate that these impulses be brought into alignment with material reality, since the claims of the biological organism are claims effectively made by the material world upon the material world. Additionally, these claims are assumed common to all individuals since they have their shared ground in the material facts of the human organism – the drives are in conflict with each other intra-psychically, but considered in the context of the organism find conceptual resolution in an underlying image of the body offered by science.

The latent essentialism of Freud's thinking about drive has played a significant role in shaping the more recent emphasis on relational context. At the same time, however, the relational emphasis on exteriority inevitably minimizes certain values that the nature of the analytic situation appears to render fundamental – e.g., the individual, self-reflection, and the freedom to choose. Ironically, while these values have sometimes come to be associated in the field with backwards conservatism, within the context of the wider society they are, more than ever, profoundly countercultural. While the relational movement has been able to garner a certain amount of radical cachet by claiming to reflect a resistance to patriarchal assumptions and the allegedly dominant values of individualism, it should be noted that contemporary ideology has little to do with the individual and a great deal more to do with the corporatism of the system (Morton, 2007, p. 101). Therefore it might be argued that the revolutionary impulse in recent psychoanalytic discourse has, to a considerable extent, inadvertently reinforced the biases of the wider society. In legitimately objecting to the role played by the drives in potentially expressing a reified conception of truth, the shift towards relational context tends to theoretically disenfranchise the individual thus opposing systemic change.

Additionally, in the absence of drives or some equivalent notion, psychoanalytic practice appears to find itself without a theory of motivation. Lacking such a theory it becomes difficult to conceive how clinicians might justify their interventions, or even explain their most rudimentary understandings of what the patient is expressing. While some phenomenologically minded figures have attempted to sidestep this problem, other relationalists have been more willing to directly acknowledge the challenge. Owing to the complications that can result otherwise, many relational theorists do not in fact go so far as to dismiss the drives completely. Ghent (1989) writes:

> The thrust of object relations theory has been to supersede Freud's objectless desire (libido as pleasure-seeking) with the formulation the libido is object-seeking. Object-seeking is seen as primary and pleasure is secondary and its detailed configuration is largely the result of experiences with objects. Now, if we allow that there is some very deep-rooted need for transcendent experience which in some way uses objects for its fulfillment, are we perhaps returning to a new version of the Freudian view of there being a need for a state of being that allows oneself to feel alive, real, changing, intense, and that usually, for this to happen an object is needed? Instead of sex as a basic drive are we not positing this need for the feeling of transcendence, or heightened aliveness as central, and that very often it is only realized in sexual context. For some people this revolutionary, transformative experience is not the one of falling in love, nor something sexual, but an intense creative drive, a mystical experience or drive, a passionate "need for power," a longing for submergence in some larger unit – all of which may be derivatives.
>
> (Ghent, 1989, p. 202)

Clearly these meaningfully charged derivatives will exert a powerful influence over the individual. As is reflected in Freud's concern with sexuality, ideas of this kind are intimately bound to the clinician's theoretical assumptions. Trilling (1982) argues that Freud founded his drive psychology with the intention of "sustaining the authenticity of human experience that formerly had been ratified by God" (p. 156). With a similar question of transcendence perhaps in mind, Ghent (1989) goes on to make the significant claim that while the experience of falling in love can be understood from a one-person perspective, love itself might be considered a two-person phenomenon (p. 203). Despite the apparent implications of this reflection, Ghent continues to conceptualize motivation as a mixture of primitive biological needs, maturational thrusts, and environment (p. 205). Thus, in Ghent's motivational thinking the role of the transpersonal remains unaddressed, and is only perhaps alluded to in an underlying commitment to conceptualize the analysand as a purposive agent rather than a mere product of circumstances.

Greenberg (1991) has also devoted considerable attention to the problem of motivation, pointedly stating: "*We cannot grasp meaning without some idea of motive*" (p. 86, italics in original). For this reason he insists that we should not shirk from asking the obvious question: "What does the child seek in seeking the object?" (p. 72). In approaching this question, Greenberg makes an important distinction between working with the notion of an endogenous force considered in the context of a psychological theory of mind, versus the notion of an endosomatic force drawn from biology. He contends that contemporary psychoanalytic theory can and must work with a concept of drive, yet should do so without reducing this notion to biology. Drives are defined by Greenberg as characteristics of mind that give rise to motivations and bring meaning to our actions. He argues that a no-drive psychology is impossible since discerning any question of meaning requires a theory of motivation, and he suggests that one-drive models fail to adequately account for the question of conflict. On this basis, Greenberg posits a dualistic drive theory intended to negotiate between the needs of safety and those of being an active participant in life, as reflected in the notion of what he terms "effectance."

While Greenberg does excellent work in arguing for the theoretical necessity of something equivalent to a drive psychology, his proposed solution is surprisingly narrow in scope. He states that multiple-drive theories are problematic since it becomes impossible to say how many drives should be recognized, and because such a model seemingly requires that the clinician adopt a naive pre-theoretical empathy so as to be able to interpret on the basis of the correct drive. These objections are questionable, in that they appear to rest upon a belief that we can somehow "choose" the number of drives in keeping with what seems theoretically practical. At the same time, in apparent contradiction to this assumption, Greenberg seems to imply that usefully interpreting from a given motivational frame of reference requires that the interpretation be "objectively" true. However, this needn't be regarded as quite so necessary if the analytic relationship is considered collaborative, and if the analyst's unavoidable theoretical assumptions about the analysand (and, by extension, the world) are necessarily to be challenged in the course of an analysis.

Nietzsche (1881/1997) cautions:

> However far a man may go in self-knowledge, nothing however can be more incomplete than his image of the totality of *drives* which constitute his being.

He can scarcely name even the cruder ones: their number and strength, their ebb and flood, their play and counterplay among one another, and above all the laws of their *nutriment* remain wholly unknown to him.

(p. 74, italics in original)

Greenberg's proposed solution fails to accommodate an effective acknowledgment of its own subjectivity. Thus, while there is surely great worth in Greenberg's initial recognition of the need to articulate our working assumptions, there appears to be something inherently problematic in his having cast his own motivational approach as though necessarily binding for others. Hoffman (1995) criticizes what he perceives to be the biases of Greenberg's approach, stating that this model is "uncritically reflective of the values of a Western, competitive, individualistic, and achievement-oriented culture" (p. 107). Hoffman endorses the notion of a multiple-drive model as a more flexible solution than the dual-drive approach which "tends to institutionalize certain values as bedrock 'human nature,' thereby immunizing them from criticism" (p. 96). Notably, however, in a subsequent publication Hoffman (1998) seems to contradict himself when he refers to the findings of his own approach in exactly the same terms – "What emerges as a kind of 'psychological bedrock,' as the immutable transcultural, transhistorical truth, is that human beings create their worlds and their sense of meaning in the teeth of the constant threat of nonbeing and meaninglessness" (p. 16). As Slavin (2001) observes, however (and reflecting the gist of Hoffman's prior criticism of Greenberg), not everyone will necessarily share Hoffman's commitment to death as a final end, nor his belief in the inherent meaninglessness of life. In having found meaning in this very meaninglessness, Hoffman comes to endorse a Sisyphean existential sensibility that is, presumably, a profound reflection of his own experience. Like Greenberg, he thus comes to endorse his own truth as necessarily binding for others.

We might be left wondering in what degree the relational approaches of Greenberg and Hoffman have really been able to challenge the essentialism more often associated with classical thinking. Despite their efforts to the contrary, in the work of both figures an underlying dogmatism emerges. Levenson (1972) thus seems justified in having earlier argued that to think in terms of purpose only succeeds in dictating to the analysand's experience in accordance with what the analyst deems important. Yet as we have seen, even in disregarding the insurmountable problems associated with an endeavor to reject motivational thinking, the constellation of the clinical situation itself already reflects foundational commitments. In seeking to respect the patient's alterity without overlooking both the ubiquitous influence of the analyst's subjectivity and the associated clinical context in which a meeting with the analyst occurs, perhaps the only coherent response is to recognize analysis as a commitment of faith which must itself be tested in the course of any given treatment. As Greenberg (1991) shows and Aron (1996) further stresses, having some form of motivational theory is inevitable.[5] The problem, then, isn't in maintaining a motivational theory (this being inevitable), but rather in holding this theory in such a way as to insufficiently recognize its status as an expression of the clinician's subjectivity. If a recognition of this kind is to be theoretically tenable, however, then the field of subjectivity must itself be empowered with a view to the theme of transcendence.

From drives to archetypes[6]

> A sane and normal society is one in which people habitually disagree, because general agreement is relatively rare outside the sphere of instinctive human qualities.
>
> (Jung, 1964, p. 46)

A different approach to motivation is needed – one that might retain the importance of the drives as signifiers of the individual, yet without falling foul of their essentialism. In light of the ethical significance Levinas attributes to the question of transcendence, a careful explication of Jung's archetypal thinking may offer an unexpectedly contemporary approach. While popularizations of Jung's ideas have often focused on the more formulaic elements of his archetypal thinking,[7] from a participatory perspective the notion of the archetype as a spiritual principle reflects an important means of conceptualizing motivation that can also accommodate alterity – a possible means of thinking about relationship that is structural, yet pluralistic and provisional in nature. Jung conceives of the archetype as a transpersonal ordering principle lying at the heart of our personal complexes. Building on Janet's concept of fixed unconscious ideas, in Jung's work the notion of the complex is used to designate a feeling-toned association of memories, ideas, and longings, which, in the expression of an underlying theme, tend to constellate in such a way as to disrupt consciousness. Addressing Jung's approach to dissociation, Frey-Rohn (1974) writes:

> In 1946 Jung finally came to the opinion that the tendency to split is a general quality of the psyche which occurs in healthy as well as in sick people. He attempted to express this idea in the concept of the dissociability of the psyche. This explanation was very important because, on the one hand, it called into question the prejudice for the unity and superiority of the ego-complex and, on the other hand, the belief in an a priori unity of the person.
>
> (p. 33)

With Jung's emphasis on the role of dissociation, the phenomenology of complexes bears a significant resemblance to what contemporary thinking understands by "self-states" (McFadden, 2012). However, while relational perspectives tend to consider self-states as internalized forms of typified interaction motivated by the underlying material needs of attachment, Jung's approach suggests that these typified interactions are structured around a transpersonal core of unrealized meaning. This archetypal kernel transcends the empirical person, yet is expressed through the structure of the personality – that is, the personal history of the individual offers the substance by means of which spirit shapes consciousness.

Owing to the extent that complexes tend to reflect the expression of typified interactions with the environment, the archetypes are considered by Jung to be the spiritual counterparts of the instincts such as to reflect "*the instinct's perception of itself,* or the self-portrait of the instinct" (Jung, 1919, para. 277, italics in original). They are regarded as the foundation of consciousness (Jung, 1959, para. 656) and as the "unconscious organizers of our ideas" (Jung, 1950, para. 278). At the same time, however, archetypes are also "locally, temporally, and individually conditioned" (Jung, 1954b, para. 476). Furthermore, they are *uniquely constellated* in each person so as to imply, in potential, the founding principles of a personal myth.[8] Jung conceptualizes the archetypes as representations of the instincts, and yet these representations are not themselves directly representable: the archetype itself is unknowable and posited (only by implication) as a dynamism, the nature of which arises in consciousness by way of images and ideas. Jung uses the spectrum of light as a metaphor, with the infrared end of the spectrum assigned to the instincts, and the ultraviolet range associated with the archetypal (Jung, 1947, para. 414). Schwartz-Salant (1986) observes:

> While Freudian approaches are personalistic (parental imagos being the main source of introverted structures), for Jung these all-important imagos are basically a form that the a priori energy of the archetype fills. The distinction is crucial in that Jung's view allows for an indigenous healing potential from within the psyche itself, whereas the other restricts healing to a restructuring of objects, internalized in childhood, by means of new introjects provided by present-day relations such as the psychotherapeutic ones.
>
> (p. 35)

Because Jung considers the archetypes to signify the possibility of a healing factor that can arise spontaneously from within as well as in relationship to others, his thinking radically affirms the importance of both the individual and the inner world. Additionally, that the archetypes are considered to be spiritual principles that are inherently unknowable seems to imply that this approach might be in keeping with the need for a way of thinking about the other such as to reflect Levinas's emphasis on transcendence. Nevertheless, it is precisely the spiritual dimension of Jung's psychology that can be most polarizing in shaping the manner in which his thinking is received. It seems that a superficial engagement with Jung's work readily enables New Age thinkers to find in it a confirmation of their own prejudices, while secularly minded psychoanalysts have historically ignored his ideas largely on the basis of hearsay. The natural association of Jung's archetypal thinking with Platonism[9] can readily give the impression that his work endorses a grand narrative model of truth concerned with legitimizing a particular take on the Beyond. Not without reason, Mills (2013) claims that Jung was primarily concerned with defending a universal theory of mind. Similarly, Brooks (2011) contends that Jung's psychology reflects a foundational ontology which she contrasts negatively to Heidegger's efforts to privilege being over knowing. She states that with the psychoid[10] concept, "Jung purported to fill in the gap between what could and what could not be known by suggesting that the noumenal might be phenomenal" (p. 501). Additionally, Brooks (2013) finds Jung's interpretive method of "amplification" incompatible with the approach of Levinas, and references the following passage from Jung (1935) as evidence of his untenable reliance on a foundationalist approach:

> The other individual has a life of his own and a mind of his own inasmuch as he is a person. But inasmuch as he is not a person, inasmuch as he is also myself, he has the same basic structure of mind, and there I can begin to think, I can associate for him. I can even provide him with the necessary context because he will have none.
>
> (para. 190)

A statement of this kind should certainly elicit skepticism. In the extent to which Jung is prone to impose a finality around the meaning of a given image or motif, such an approach seems no longer credible. Clearly, though, if amplification is understood in a softer sense as expressing a playful relationship to the patient's material similar to Bion's notion of reverie, then Jung's outlook may appear less categorically objectionable in the context of an ethics of the other.[11] In the extent to which Jung seeks to emphasize the fundamentally unknowable nature of the archetype itself, Marlan (2005) argues that his theoretical approach in fact bears comparison with the postmodern practice of *sous rature*.[12] Furthermore, just as Jung's work can be argued to point towards an outlook that significantly problematizes his status as a foundationalist, Levinas's work can be argued to leave room for the possibility of establishing some measure of systematicity in relationship to the other. Certainly Levinas is careful to argue that endorsing the notion of transcendence does not require a reinstating of metaphysics – his approach posits transcendence in an avowedly ethical frame of reference that is not concerned with uncovering hidden principles but rather in engaging with what he terms: "a *spiritual intrigue wholly other than gnosis*" (Levinas, 1984/1997, p. 154, italics in original). In its most extreme expression, Levinas's ethical sensibility requires that the other be approached as an abstraction with which we can imagine nothing in common, thus necessitating an assumption of absolute difference (Levinas, 1962/1997, p. 27). But how credible is this approach in claiming to avoid an underlying metaphysic? As Ricoeur (1986) observes: "If the forbidding of murder is not based on force, to what ultimate foundation may we appeal, if not the absolutes of Justice and Peace, manifested by the face?" (p. 456). Similarly, Purcell (2003) contends that while Levinas is naturally averse to theology's tendency to systematize and circumscribe the Absolute, his work still points to the possibility of developing an ethically inspired fundamental theology. Jung and Levinas may, therefore, be a good deal more reconcilable than might initially be assumed.

While there is much in Jung's work suggesting that his approach is too conservative to support a postmodern ethics of the other, a reading of this kind doesn't address the full scope of his thinking. In particular, it fails to recognize the extent to which his work comes to express a participatory worldview, the nuances of which are generally not appreciated. Jung (1951) writes:

A kind of fluid interpenetration belongs to the very nature of all archetypes. They can only be roughly circumscribed at best. Their living meaning comes out more from their presentation as a whole than from a single formulation. Every attempt to focus them more sharply is immediately punished by the intangible core of meaning losing its luminosity. No archetype can be reduced to a simple formula. It is a vessel which we can never empty, and never fill. It has a potential existence only, and when it takes shape in matter it is no longer what it was. It persists throughout the ages and requires interpreting ever anew. The archetypes are the imperishable elements of the unconscious, but they change their shape continually.

(para. 301)

Drawing from statements of this kind, Tarnas (2006) reads Jung as perceiving the archetypes to be "universal essences or forms at once intrinsic to and independent of the human mind, that not only endure as timeless universals but are also cocreatively enacted and recursively affected through human participation" (p. 86). Tarnas (2012) suggests that the archetypes can be conceived as immanent and dynamically enacted in a fashion similar to Aristotle's universals, but also as transcendent universal principles more in keeping with the notion of Platonic forms. Though the archetypes are frequently portrayed by Jung in such a way as to leave the reader assuming that they are eternally binding principles, or at the very least the ancient precipitates of biological evolution, in his late work Jung (1954a) gives the impression that the conscious efforts of humanity in the present moment can be understood to result in corresponding shifts in the nature of the transpersonal psyche.

The indeterminate quality of the archetypal domain is reflected conceptually in the unsystematic fashion in which Jung portrays his thinking on the matter. In seeking clarification, it should be noted that, as Hogenson (2004) observes, "Jung did not have a theory of archetypes" (p. 33). It might therefore be recognized that Jung's work has invited so much commentary partly because of its suggestive and *necessarily* inconclusive nature.[13] That the archetypes are characterized by Jung as transcendent has been significantly minimized in the recent development of his work. Owing to the contemporary intellectual climate, this dimension of his psychology has been difficult to support. As a consequence, considerable effort has been exerted by some Jungians to try to ground the archetypes in a conventional biological framework (e.g., Stevens, 1982; Goodwyn, 2012). This approach to Jung's thinking claims that since the instincts must be considered a product of biological evolution, so too are the archetypes:

The basis of ethology is the recognition that an instinct must be understood in terms of a species' environment of evolutionary adaptedness, that is, the environment in which it has evolved and to which that instinct has served to adapt the species. This is the context in which we may explain the purpose of an instinct (that is, its adaptive function). [...] Therefore, to understand the purpose (adaptive function) of the archetypes (as the psychical correlate of the instincts), we must consider Homo sapiens' environment of evolutionary adaptedness.

(MacLennan, 2006, pp. 11–12)

This seemingly reasonable position is, upon closer inspection, arguably backwards. Since the archetypes are posited to structure meaning, it seems incoherent to speak of them having a "purpose" – any notion of purpose is itself by definition an archetypal construct. While from an evolutionary perspective the archetypes are indeed the precipitate of the instincts, this holds true only from within the confines of this archetypal meaning construct. Freud's (1915a) often less ambiguous emphasis on the body causes him to construe the drives as "the demand made upon the mind for work in consequence of its connection with the body" (p. 122). The meaning of the drive is thus imposed upon it out of the assumptions of biology, and reduced to the theme of pleasure satisfaction. Jung, by contrast, seems to imply that we cannot get a clear read on the meaning of our motivations since such an undertaking is itself always motivated. Furthermore, because each person structures meaning in their own irreducibly unique way, in a significant sense we each can only be expected to express our own truth. Even so, this truth might be understood as the unfolding in time of something transpersonal.

With reference to Jung's assertions that the archetypes were formed out of lived experience, Rensma (2013) has convincingly demonstrated that Jung's work often flirts with Lamarckian ideas, and that the efforts of biologically inclined Jungians to "defend" Jung against the suggestion that his psychology does not fit neatly into a strictly Darwinian paradigm are unconvincing. In fact, the Lamarckian strain sometimes detectable in Jung's work is by no means the most challenging aspect of his approach to the matter – his archetypal thinking perhaps threatens to burst the confines of the evolutionary paradigm altogether. Recognition of this tendency, however, requires an attentive attitude to the logic of Jung's thinking, and a willingness to follow this logic to its conclusion. The archetypes are representations of the instincts, yet these representations are not themselves directly representable. This might leave us wondering what the instincts actually are. Since they can only be brought into consciousness by way of the archetypes (which are themselves fundamentally unknowable), it seems impossible to say. Thus, while the instinctual might be assumed primary by a biologist, to remain within a psychological frame of reference, even speaking of the instinctual requires that we have an idea of it, and to have a meaningful idea of it, consciousness is already being constellated around archetypal influences. The instincts are therefore at a double remove from consciousness; we infer their existence only with recourse to the representations (what Jung refers to as archetypal images) of their representations (the archetypes per se).[14] As Manfred Frank (1997) observes on a related note: "Bodily properties first acquire the meaning through which they disclose themselves intersubjectively to the linguistic community from individual interpretations, and thus cannot in turn condition the latter" (p. 23).

An approach of this kind suggests that, contrary to expectations, emphasizing the more esoteric aspects of Jung's work may in fact result in an outlook with more relevance to contemporary practice than emerges from seeking to subject his ideas to a reductive reading in terms of biology. Analytical psychology has been upheld for the most part in clinical rather than academic environs, thus the trajectory of Jungian thinking has been made subject to a possibly counter-productive demand for mainstream clinical respectability. Additionally, Jung's own desire to identify himself as a scientist alongside his reticence to directly engage with the metaphysical implications of his work has left his psychology vulnerable to scientistic reduction. The diminishing that Jung's ideas have sometimes undergone as a consequence is nowhere more evident than in the recent trend towards "supporting" his work with recourse to the speculative assumptions of evolutionary biology.[15] While this trend has reached a new apotheosis in the fetishizing of neuroscience, the groundwork for this tendency was perhaps established with the genetic approach of Erich Neumann. Neumann's (1954) magnum opus, *The Origins and History of Consciousness*, purports to outline the evolution of consciousness as expressed through a proposed historical development of mythology. In this fashion, Neumann effectively seeks to offer a universally binding history of the archetypes. Giegerich (1975) mounts a strong critique of Neumann's project, arguing that Neumann's history suffers from a chronic lack of historically dateable material, and that a study of mythology refutes the proposed chronology. More fundamentally, however, Giegerich reminds us that the evolutionary perspective rests upon a form of religious fascination that marks this perspective as itself being archetypal (p. 27), hence attempting to explain the entire archetypal field from this singular perspective is inherently problematic.[16]

Remaining faithful to a psychological perspective, with a careful reading of Jung we can no longer assume that the instincts have epistemological priority. While this conclusion might disappoint those who would seek to position Jung as a pioneer in evolutionary psychology, it is nonetheless in keeping with his claim that physical reality is a postulate, and materialism a hypostasis of matter (Jung, 1939, para. 762 & 765). This aspect of Jung's thinking also resonates to a considerable degree with Lacan,[17] who is likewise concerned to problematize the relationship between "the body" and our experience of it. Lacan suggests that the body is infiltrated by the symbolic realm having been written over with signifiers in the acquisition of language. While it may seem counter-intuitive to claim that our experience of the body is not basic, this idea is also expressed in Freud's (1915b) notion of primal repression: "a first phase of repression, which consists in the psychically [ideational] representative of the instinct being denied entrance into the conscious" (p. 148). Developing Freud's thinking, Lacan (1954–55/1991) claims that "Freudian biology has nothing to do with biology" (p. 75), and that the reality of the body is something that comes to be irreversibly obscured as we enter language. This establishes a dynamic in his theorizing reminiscent of Jung, in that Lacan's postulating of the register of the real as an inexpressible order lying beyond language is itself posited by way of language, and hence is subject to the same problematizing apparent in Jung's approach to the instincts and their inference by way of the archetype. In both cases, any pursuit of a final truth lying beyond the meanings we construe culminates in an uroboric swallowing of the tail.[18] A recognition of this pursuit lies at the heart of a participatory metaphysics. For Jung, the transpersonal dimension of experience is registered in active participation with the process of meaning-making, or in "dreaming the myth forward" (Jung, 1951, p. 160), which for Lacan is registered by a shift in the individual's relationship to the wider symbolic order as expressed in a radical disruption to the fundamental fantasy. Lacan (1959–60/1997) emphasizes an approach to the psyche that postulates a-temporal structures rather than stages of linear development. His notion of retroaction (an expansion of Freud's "deferred action") suggests that the past is only meaningfully constituted in the present, leading him to state quite unequivocally: "beware of that register of thought known as evolutionism" (para. 213).

In Freud's thinking, the notion of the repression barrier effectively prevents the self-conscious subject from being able to achieve a direct recognition of their own motivations. Emphasizing this idea in support of a classical position, Barratt (2013) appears to be drawing inspiration from Lacan when he claims that "psychoanalysis asserts the primacy of desire over existence" such that "desire animates each of us seemingly endlessly and far more powerfully than does our semiotic comprehension of consensual realities" (p. 24). In offering this position, he cites Forrester's (1990) significant observation that for Freud *repetition is prior to origination*. In emphasizing a participatory/uroboric reading of the archetypes, the significance of this idea is returned to its original philosophical context. For Schelling (1813/1997), a notion equivalent to primal repression is made necessary as a consequence of the philosophical need to account for the subject's freedom from causal determination:

> This is how things had to stand if there were to be an eternal beginning, an eternal ground. That primordial deed which makes a man genuinely himself precedes all individual actions; but immediately after it is put into exuberant freedom, this deed sinks into the night of unconsciousness. This is not a deed that could happen once then stop; it is a permanent deed, a never-ending deed, and consequently it can never again be brought before consciousness.
>
> (p. 181)

Establishing a fundamental fissure between self and world, primal repression is conceived in this frame of reference as a metaphysical gesture – a founding act which posits the unconscious as the originary ground upon which the emergence of the subject depends. Building on the idea that self-consciousness can never gain transparency owing to the inevitable repudiation of desire, a participatory approach might seek to understand this idea in the transpersonal context of Schelling's metaphysic of the unconscious and in this way to more directly challenge the Freudian temptation to reify origins in an image of the body offered by science. In maintaining the transcendent ground of consciousness as such, a more self-reflexive basis seems to be offered from which to begin to articulate motivation – an approach which refrains from reductively shackling itself to an objective ontology and the endeavor to support current scientific conceptions of reality. With an archetypal approach to participation, in its indeterminate obscurity the unconscious only becomes accessible to conscious interpretation by way of subjectively embodied experience.

In contrast to the assumption that Jung's archetypal thinking promotes a naive and philosophically dated mode of spiritual essentialism, a participatory reading of his ideas points to a destabilizing and existentially nuanced concept of transcendence. From a participatory perspective, in the very effort to approach origins in the search for meaning, these origins are themselves made subject to change. It is something of this kind that Jung (1921) appears to evoke when he speaks of "the noumenon of the image which intuition perceives and, in perceiving, creates" (para. 659).[19] Rather than promoting a naive religious revivalism, the challenging and unstable nature of these ideas can in fact seem like a threat to spiritual psychology. Transpersonal theorist Ken Wilber's sometimes aggressive diatribes against post-structuralism and what he terms "the rancid leveling of all qualitative distinctions" (p. 160) is suggestive of this. Wilber (2000) writes: "The extreme postmodernists do not just stress the importance of interpretation, they claim reality is nothing but an interpretation" (p. 163). From a participatory perspective, however, the notion that reality is founded in interpretation need not imply that there is nothing resembling an objective situation, but simply that the objective situation is enacted participatorily and hence is subject to change.

Wilber's tendency to rely on developmental thinking has reflected a wider trend within transpersonal psychology to normalize spirituality. Ferrer (2002) writes:

> The esotericist claims that mystics of all ages and places converge about metaphysical matters is a dogma that cannot be sustained by the evidence. In contrast to the perennialist view, what the spiritual history of humankind suggests is that spiritual doctrines and intuitions affected, shaped, and transformed each other, and that this mutual influence led to the unfolding of a variety of metaphysical worlds – rather than to one metaphysic and different languages.
>
> (p. 94)

Reflecting a more conventional approach to transpersonal thinking, Combs (2002) argues:

> Just how flexible, however, can reality be? Is it just putty to be molded into any shape whatsoever? Few would argue for this position, though certain postmodern constructionist thinkers seem to flirt with it. A more likely position is that reality is only incompletely defined in terms readily understood by nervous systems. In this case the principal occupation of science and philosophy is to sharpen up its corners for us, grinding the right set of lenses through which to see it truly.
>
> (Combs, 2002, p. 55)

This attitude appears to be more in keeping with the perspectival assumptions of much relational thinking. For figures like Jung and Lacan, by contrast, it is imperative that we recognize how the nervous system is already implicated in the meaning-making process. There is no question of separating the data of the senses from our interpretation of it.

Far from being adapted to the environment, Lacan (1966/2005) feels that humanity is dis-adapted as a consequence of being born prematurely: "man's relation to nature is altered by a certain dehiscence at the heart of the organism" (p. 78). In a similar vein, Sullivan writes: "Don't permit yourself to think that the animal can be discovered after it has been modified by the incorporation of culture: it is no longer there. It is not a business of a social personality being pinned on or spread over a human animal" (Sullivan, 1950, p. 210). Thinking in this way does not require that we dismiss conceptions of the body or the legitimacy of the biological sciences on their own terms, but it does entail remaining committed to a psychological frame of reference and thus understanding the body as psychically constituted.[20] For psychodynamic clinicians this means having the courage of our professional convictions and making the individual primary, rather than knowingly dictating to the experience of the subject on the basis of imported assumptions as to the nature of our biology.

Towards a pluralistic structuralism

> Metaphysics is formed in the spontaneous thinking of every human being, prior to any possible formulation in the language of theory.
>
> (Henrich, 1987b, p. 14)[21]

> The things of heaven and earth contain such a wealth of value that only the organs of all beings jointly can encompass it.
>
> (Goethe, 1813/1949, p. 46)

In order to appreciate something of the intent behind Jung's archetypal thinking, it is helpful to return to the context – or in Henrich's sense, the *Denkraum* – of the early field. The so-called "personal equation" constituted a central preoccupation for late nineteenth- and early twentieth-century psychology. This term was originally coined in the field of astronomy, where it was used to connote the sometimes significant mathematical problems arising as a consequence of subtle imprecisions in measurement. Shamdasani (2004) states that William James played a significant role in bringing this notion to the discipline of psychology, in which context it presented a major obstacle to establishing the field along properly scientific lines. While the hard sciences could respond convincingly to this problem by introducing statistical methods of controlling for error, in so far as psychology concerned itself with phenomena that were not directly observable, the personal equation signified a major obstacle. Introspectionism would be abandoned in the early twentieth century largely because introspective psychologists were unable to come to any sort of consensus as to how the content of experience should be analyzed. Thus the attempt to structurally account for the nature of consciousness was rendered a failure owing to the diversity of reported experiences. In the early history of psychoanalysis, it was effectively hoped that the personal equation could be controlled for by means of the training analysis. Unfortunately, this solution only resulted in an intellectual climate in which differences of opinion frequently devolved into mutual accusations of psychopathology.

Clearly the pathologizing of theoretical divergences threatened to make a farce of psychoanalytic discourse. The vehemence with which received ideas were protected was often cruel in its consequences. Those that defected, sometimes under traumatic personal circumstances, were perhaps better positioned in their experience to at least attempt to address this problem in a more open-minded fashion. Adler (1938), the first of the major figures to break with Freud, would go on to develop the notion that a person's behavior is controlled by an underlying idea about the nature of reality that comes to be expressed in what he refers to as a "style of life." He stresses that a person is influenced not by the facts themselves, but by their interpretation of them. Adler perceives that the individual is required to bring his or her own style of life into the service of social norms. In approaching clinical work, Adler thus asserts that analysts should have recourse to sociology in identifying and affirming the tasks of living which he considers to be a given fact of our existence. Although this approach demonstrates a considerable effort to incorporate the personal equation, it seems clear that Adler fails to recognize his conception of the tasks of living and the psychology he postulates in responding to them are inevitably a reflection of his own style of life – this should come as little surprise least of all to Adler himself, who appears to argue that we cannot in fact gain the reflective distance that would be required to grasp the idea we have of ourselves and the world (pp. 26–27). Thus, while acknowledging that each individual strives to bring to fulfillment his or her own life's goal, Adler comes to perceive in each person's goal the reflection of Adler's own controlling idea of perfection.[22]

Shamdasani (2004) explores the extent to which Jung's earlier work on typology reflects an effort to overcome the personal equation. With particular reference to Jung's correspondence with Hans Schmid, Shamdasani shows that prior even to the publication of his psychological typology, Jung expressed serious doubts as to whether an objective system of personality classification was really conceivable (p. 70). Despite these concerns, Jung still came to promote a system that portrays the personality as falling into one of eight typical configurations, each of which reflects a tendency to experience the world in a particular way. Jung's typology is thus suggestive of the parable of the blind men and the elephant – each man, feeling a different part of the same elephant, comes to a very different opinion about the kind of creature standing before them. In this parable, the elephant itself exists as an independent whole, the different parts of which are grasped by means of the subjectivities encountering it. Jung seeks to circumvent the personal equation by offering his typology as a means to acquiring a complete picture of the elephant.[23]

While largely putting aside his work with typology subsequent to the publication of *Psychological Types*, Jung's highly nuanced development of the idea of the archetypes in his later writings points to his lasting engagement with the personal equation. In as much as the founding of a properly scientific psychology in his earlier work seemed to depend on Jung overcoming the personal factor, self-reflexively incorporating this question into the substance of his later theorizing was perhaps the more fruitful challenge. Jung's thinking about the archetypes stresses that their influence in structuring meaning tends to be reflected in a particular gestalt. For Jung, the archetypes can never be decontextualized and thus observed in their raw form, nor can they be considered as discretely organized[24] – we are no longer dealing with parts of the one elephant but, in a sense, with as many manifestations of the elephant as there are blind men encountering it. His archetypal thinking therefore appears to offer a means of conceptualizing how we might approach a metaphysics of subjectivity without forgoing the influence of postmodern thinking. This notion corresponds with Ferrer and Sherman's (2008) contention that the idea of participatory enaction theoretically makes conceivable the creation of as many metaphysical or religious worlds as there are forms of self-disclosure. They state:

> Granting the indisputable holism of religious meanings, we suggest that this holism is not logically inconsistent with the possibility that such meanings may possess ontological or metaphysical referents. If we allow for the plausibility of a multiplicity of actual religious worlds capable of referentially anchoring a number of religious meanings, we can coherently affirm both contextuality and the supratextual import of many significant religious traditions.

(p. 25)

The participatory approach to archetypal thinking outlined here is reflected in the fundamental question that drew Jung (1963a) into confrontation with himself: *what is the myth I am living?* From a clinical perspective this question can be considered essential, since for the analyst it is intimately associated with asking: *what is the motivational model with which I am working?* For Jung, the individual brings into being a world that is contextually defined in transcendence. Nevertheless, the extent to which Jung's approach succeeds in enabling others to engage their own myth has perhaps been partially hampered as a consequence of the extent to which Jung's own answer to this question is also expressed in his work, and by how this answer has sometimes been carried forward by his interpreters so as to obscure the underlying existential challenge otherwise posed. Jung's particular emphasis on individuation as the quest to achieve wholeness has been widely adopted by many Jungians, yet it is questionable in what degree this outlook can still accommodate the more open-ended question of the personal myth.

Guggenbuhl-Craig (1980) points out that Jung's focus on wholeness inevitably leaves out invalidism and a recognition of pathology and incompleteness. James Hillman attempts to address this bias through his own psychology, offering a phenomenological/aesthetic approach to the archetypes that naturally comes to reflect something of Hillman's own myth. Hillman (1983) states that: "unlike Jung, who radically distinguishes between noumenal archetype *per se* and phenomenal archetypal image, archetypal psychology [the term Hillman adopts in reference to his own approach] rigorously refuses even to speculate about a non-presented archetype *per se*" (p. 21). Influenced by Christou (1963), Hillman's rhetorical approach seeks to define the spiritual perspective in opposition to the ideal of fantasy which he perceives to reflect the essence of a psychological outlook. However, in discounting spirit Hillman's psychology refuses to acknowledge its own foundations and can thus potentially degenerate into its own form of reductivism (Brown, 2014a). As a consequence of this lack of tolerance for the spiritual stance, it is perhaps unsurprising that Hillman's later thought threatens to fall back into the materialism that it sought to avoid – in connection with the emergence of ecopsychology he goes so far as to directly identify the collective unconscious with the material world itself (Hillman, 1995), thus potentially collapsing the very distinction upon which his own emphasis on fantasy rests.[25]

In the effort to revise the specifics of Jung's approach, the extent to which Hillman's psychology comes to express its own commitments is revealing. Clearly the endeavor to establish a psychology is always subject to personal coloration. Therefore, in so far as possible the participatory approach to archetypal thinking being offered in the present context is offered as the articulation of an outlook that might provide clinicians with a more effective means of holding their own commitments, rather than as a fully formed psychology in its own right. Such an approach posits a way to think about motivation without reifying it – an attitude that encourages the clinician to hold their own commitments with the seriousness they demand, yet without assuming these commitments to be universally binding. At the same time, it is essential that this holding approach to motivational theory be understood as itself reflecting commitments *in* theory. Owing to the field's grounding in praxis, however, the basis for these commitments might be considered in a significant sense already given by virtue of the clinical situation itself – every working analyst is effectively committed from the outset owing to their choice of profession. It is therefore suggested that the question of theoretical foundations should be grounded in the nature of the clinical situation and the fundamental commitment to the subject which is posited to emerge from this in light of the challenges of pluralism. The limits of psychoanalysis as a pluralistic discourse are necessarily given by virtue of practice. Psychodynamic treatment thus comes to reflect a trial of the analyst's professional faith, as expressed in the effort to facilitate the other.

In keeping with such an outlook, Henrich argues that the philosophy of subjectivity needn't require a fixed metaphysics, and that a metaphysical project can be maintained without the need of certainty. The subject depends on a transcendent ground – a ground which distances itself from conventional religious thinking in the extent to which institutionalized approaches to the spirit tend to privilege particular structures of subjectivity. Approaches of this kind are considered by Henrich to be no longer tenable owing to their failure to address the question of self-reflexivity that characterizes modernity. As Freundlieb (2003) puts it: "The concept of the Unconditioned now becomes dependent on specific conceptions of the world. With the beginning of modernity God has to be renamed as the Absolute" (p. 75). In Henrich's view, the philosophy of subjectivity inevitably engenders metaphysical questions that cannot be answered by science or our everyday conceptions of the world. Rather than emphasizing the notion of mastery, Henrich suggests that the recognition of subjectivity might be understood as summoning the question of conflict with others such as to give rise to the need of establishing commonality. In this light, the metaphysical impulse demonstrates a concern for unity that can be considered reconciliatory rather than necessarily domineering.

For Henrich, the organization of mind is regarded as an active process that draws us into life. In offering a philosophy that is potentially transformative for consciousness and that provides some sense of basic existential orientation, Henrich returns to classical German philosophy in support of his efforts to endorse a non-foundationalist metaphysics. The viability of such a project is reflected in Pinkard's (2002) statement that post-Kantian idealism culminates in a recognition that, as self-legislated, "our normative authority is always open to challenge, which means that 'we' are always open to challenge; and that the only challenges that can count are contained within the 'infinite' activity of giving and asking for reasons" (p. 367). In keeping with this claim, Henrich endorses the notion that the speculative nature of metaphysical thinking helps register our subjective assumptions more clearly.

Post-Kantian idealism suggests that conscious life is structured by means of certain conflictual tendencies, each tending to generate a particular world image. Fichte famously argues that "idealism" and "dogmatism" are two systems that oppose each other without hope that one can refute the other. In light of this claim, Fichte (1982) states:

> What sort of philosophy one chooses depends, therefore, on what sort of man one is; for a philosophical system is not a dead piece of furniture that we can reject or accept as we wish; it is rather a thing animated by the soul of the person who holds it.
>
> (p. 6)

Schleiermacher goes on to address this problem by positing the incommensurability of our core intuitions, thus establishing the basis for a religious pluralism that gave rise to the discipline of hermeneutics. Similarly, for Novalis, the conditions for knowledge are established in a particular form of self-consciousness that he calls "feeling," and which has the epistemic form of "faith" (Frank, 1995b, p. 75). In late career, Schelling would also introduce his notion of "positive" philosophy wherein metaphysical postulates could be asserted and explored without requiring rational justification since reason is itself understood to be just one such of these postulates. Henrich (1987a) cites Holderlin's distinction between three different approaches to life: the quest for self-perfection, the pursuit of beauty, and the commonality of being. Drawing from Holderlin, Henrich's approach to the epistemic self-relation engenders a recognition that multiple ontologies exist each of which brings about a different relationship to life:

> Our life is such that conflicting tendencies (active principles) of conduct and orientation emerge from it and gain equally justified persuasive power.

Analyzing life in terms of these conflicts was a possibility discovered by post-Kantian philosophy. It also showed that each of these tendencies tends to generate a description of a human world in which a life that is dominated and oriented by a particular tendency can be conceived of as being at home and at peace within it. These descriptions or world-images are therefore engaged in the very same conflict and exclude each other as completely as the tendencies themselves. [...] Tendencies like these are not reducible to one another. They are equally primordial and intrinsically stabilized by virtue of a metaphysical world image. They can only become reconciled through a second-level insight into their origin, the inevitability of their conflict and the likelihood that any life will founder which tries to remain blindly faithful to the guidance of one of the tendencies once it has been adopted.

(Henrich, 1987a, p. 119)

Henrich is hesitant in the extent to which we might achieve this form of second-order insight or negotiate between conflicting images of the world. In classical psychoanalysis, a striving of this kind has traditionally been reflected in the reconciliatory function of the ego. Richard Sterba (1934) describes a therapeutic split between the observing ego and the experiencing ego − a split which is perceived as necessary for the analysand to assume a standpoint considered in some sense "outside" of immediate experience. The assumptions attendant to this model of subjectivity have been substantially challenged by the more recent emphasis on the self's pluralism. Just as thinking in terms of self-states has helped undermine the notion of a monolithic subject, Jung's emphasis on the personal myth offers an approach to the world images Henrich speaks of that indicates the restrictions of insight. An appreciation for the self-reflexive nature of any attempt to interpret the archetypal ground of motivation is essential, for it establishes a fundamental epistemic uncertainty in our world-views. Significantly, however, this uncertainty is posited without demeaning the status of the insights thus attained − in fact, unmodulated experiences normally deemed pathological can now potentially be understood to disclose particular images of the world that are inevitably colored in the effort to achieve a second-order perception.

While the archetypal field can never be grasped in itself, Jung (1958) still retains some hope of working around the limits of the personal equation:

The present day shows with appalling clarity how little able people are to let the other man's argument count, although this capacity is a fundamental and indispensable condition for any human community. Everyone who proposes to come to terms with himself must reckon with this basic problem. For, to the degree that he does not admit the validity of the other person, he denies the "other" within himself the right to exist − and vice versa. The capacity for inner dialogue is a touchstone for outer objectivity.

(para. 187)

Through the process of active imagination, Jung envisages that establishing a dialogue with ourselves (reflecting something of the shifting relationships between our organizing principles) the possibility arises of meeting the other on an objective basis. The nature of this so-called objectivity, however, needn't be quite so epistemically dubious as it sounds. Objectivity in this sense can be understood to denote the individual's capacity to actively encounter the other, so that the emergence of truth is conceived in terms of engaging a process rather than in taking hold of a concrete fact. This reflects Jung's (1921) emphasis on respecting the legitimacy of "psychological facts" which, by virtue of their subjectivity, must be considered inherently fluid. In a similar light, Henrich (1982) states:

> "Truth" does not mean in this context scientifically guaranteed knowledge. The human being recognizes as true what has the most comprehensive self-evidence and opens up the most illuminating perspectives. And this is not a truth "as if", with the reservation that we cannot help but think like that, but the strongest affirmation in actual conscious life of which a human being is capable. In this sense the great interpretations of life were certainly true.
>
> (p. 31)

In referencing this passage, Dews (1996) points out that the position outlined also exhibits parallels with Charles Taylor's claim that the moral sources of the self cannot finally be proven, but must be fallibilistically accepted as the best account currently available (p. 192). Drawing on the history of classical German philosophy out of which psychodynamic psychiatry emerged, a participatory approach to Jung's archetypal thinking suggests that this question of fallibilism needn't require weak-form constructivism's capitulation to an objective ontology.

CODA: PSYCHOTHERAPY AS A CATALYST FOR COLLECTIVE CHANGE

The uncertainty of the mind and that of the real offer both risks and opportunities. The insufficiency of immediate realism opens the door to what lies beyond the immediate. The problem is to be neither realistic in the trivial sense (to adapt to the immediate), nor unrealistic in the trivial sense (to exclude oneself from the constraints of reality), but to be realistic in a complex sense (to comprehend the uncertainty of reality, to know that there are possibilities still invisible in the real), which often seems unrealistic. Here again, reality eludes the realists and utopians alike.

(Morin, 1999, p. 108)[1]

The political and spiritual dimensions of psychoanalytic discourse have been fundamentally shaped by Freud's notion of the reality principle. This continues to be reflected in the core assumptions of the relational movement. Ian Hacking (1999) notes that most constructivists are more concerned with addressing political questions than metaphysical ones (p. 58). In keeping with this observation, relational thinking has tended to emphasize the notion of social adaptation over self-realization. The French philosopher Gilbert Simondon is critical of such an emphasis, drawing attention to how the individual tends to get lost in the process. He argues in favor of a trans-individualism such that, in going beyond his or herself, the person embraces an aspect of eternity and in so doing experiences authentic communion with others. Simondon states: "knowledge's *conditions of possibility* are identical with the individuated being's *causes of existence*" (cited in Scott, 2014, p. 20, italics in original).

In the work of Russian religious and political philosopher Nikolai Berdyaev, creative freedom is conceived as transcendent and necessarily inexplicable: "In his essence, man is a break in the world of nature, he cannot be contained within it" (Berdyaev, 1954, p. 62). Berdyaev is careful to show how this notion of creative freedom is not to be confused with an escapist individualism. Perhaps recalling Fichte's distinction between dogmatism and idealism, Berdyaev likewise argues that there are two varieties of philosophy: the kind that asserts the primacy of being over freedom, and the kind that asserts the primacy of freedom over being. Correspondingly, there are two tendencies of the human spirit, neither one of which can afford to be overlooked: adaptation to necessity, and the creative assertion of freedom. The individual is required to consciously orient his or her self to the world and thus come into correspondence with its realities – an estrangement from the world, in so far as this would reflect a refusal to recognize given realities, inevitably leads to our becoming enslaved to it (p. 152). Nevertheless, Berdyaev still insists that in a spiritual climate where the positivist worldview has gained such dominance, "all philosophy must pass through the heroic act of denying 'the truth'" (p. 44). This commitment to life in refutation of its disclosed reality is portrayed as a creative act of overcoming that can ultimately effect a change in the collective itself.

It was suggested in the previous chapter that contemporary psychoanalysis must affirm the notion of transcendence if it is to remain tenable as a basis for pluralistic therapy, for only in so doing can it be hoped that the analysand's experience might come to be valued as genuinely revelatory. When considering our theoretical tools, the implicit value accorded to the individual is paramount if we are to avoid adopting restrictive modes of perceiving the analysand. Charles and O'Loughlin (2012) observe that constrictive views of mental illness result in isolating the afflicted, thus exacerbating suffering (p. 411). If we set out with an assumption that the individual is merely an expression of the material conditions from which he or she arises, then the patient's experience is inevitably demeaned as a mere epiphenomenon of genetics and/or social conditioning. By contrast, if we posit that the individual is motivated by factors transcending material causes, then it becomes conceivable that the individual's experience may carry a meaning for the material situation that is not immediately reducible to it. In keeping with such a view, Maurice Blondel (1893/1984) argues that human action always suggests a transcendent goal, so that motivation exceeds its apparent aim (p. 358). Only by understanding others in these terms can the possibility of a genuine clinical respect emerge. Such a respect necessarily entails a very different way of thinking about the kind of change that psychoanalysis might strive to promote.

Substance and change[2]

> Without a present that is determined and definite, there is no [past at all]; how many have the privilege of such a past? The man who cannot separate himself from himself, who cannot break loose from everything that happens to him and actively oppose it – such a man has no past, or more likely he never emerges from it, but lives in it continually. It is advantageous and beneficial for a man to be conscious of having put something behind him, as it were – that is, of having posited it as past.
>
> (Schelling, 1813/1997, p. 120)

Following a participatory line of thinking, Owen Barfield (1988) argues: "if the particles, or the unrepresented, are in fact all that is *independently* there, then the world we all accept as real is in fact a system of collective representations" (p. 20, italics in original). Reflecting on the nature of the historical enterprise, Barfield notices that received opinion proceeds on the mistaken assumption that in the past "the unrepresented was behaving in such a way that, if human beings with the collective representations characteristic of the last few centuries of western civilization had been there, the things described would also have been there" (p. 37). Considered in terms of the individual, this line of thinking has interesting implications for the mainstream assumption that therapeutic practice is concerned merely with trans-forming how we think about the material facts of the past. Following Barfield, we might consider that "history" has no meaning outside of our shared experience of it, hence a change in the experiential dimension is indistinguishable from a change in the historical actuality. This position is reflected also in the thinking of Alfred North Whitehead (1926):

> It is a curious delusion that the rock upon which our beliefs can be founded is an historical investigation. You can only interpret the past in terms of the present. The present is all that you have; and unless in this present you can find general principles which interpret the present as including a representation of the whole community of existents, you cannot move a step beyond your little patch of immediacy.
>
> Thus history presupposes a metaphysic. It can be objected that we believe in the past and talk about it without settling our metaphysical principles. That is certainly the case. But you can only deduce metaphysical dogmas from your interpretation of the past on the basis of a prior metaphysical interpretation of the present.
>
> (p. 84)

Exhortations to "live in the now" have become a cliché of pop psychology. Unfortunately, this particular injunction can readily come to serve as a shorthand for the repression of the individual in service to social norms. In this case "living in the now" is understood quite literally, as though in distinction to living in the past or future. This appears nonsensical, however, since it seems clear that a preoccupation with such matters cannot be said to literally place a person outside of the present moment. Where a therapist encourages a client to move away from fantasies of the past or future, far from fostering an engagement with the present what is actually striven for is quite the opposite: rather than accepting the present for what it is, the effect is to actively reject it in favor of something deemed more "useful." In other words, by the very quality of its striving the therapist's approach is, by definition, oriented towards a future of *their* own determining, and in fact neglects much of the patient's present altogether. This also has implications for the notion of "recovery," a word which itself seems to suggest the question of returning to a prior state of concealment − *keeping a lid on it.*

Clearly the historical record should not be confused with any idea we might have of the past as an objective fact, for the past exists only as a function of the present. Jodorowsky (2010) asserts: "Son and mother are connected psychically. If the mother had not made a step in the direction of adopting a different attitude [...] the son would feel it, even if he were far away" (p. 84). This is perhaps suggestive of the effect that a shift in individual consciousness is sometimes claimed to have upon others close to them – an expression of the family systems notion that even absent relatives are as much a part of the collective dynamic as those more outwardly present. While the creative dynamism of the psyche tends to be regarded only in terms of the effect it might have on the future, the subject of creation is just as much the past. This past, in so far as configured in the unconscious constellation of meaning, must itself be considered susceptible to change since the past will always be reflective of our relationship to the present. An outlook of this kind was fore-shadowed with Freud's shift from uncovering the truth of a seduction to the emphasis on fantasy.

A participatory outlook offers a new basis from which to appreciate the seeming magnitude of the task of forgiveness. Remaining wed to a positivist paradigm, the status of fantasy in Freud's thinking often elicits anger wherever it is felt that such a position demeans the reality of trauma and the suffering consequent upon it. By relinquishing our theoretical attachment to what really happened, however, this criticism need no longer apply; the reality of what took place is expressed precisely in its unshakable impact on how we imagine the world and our place in it. This frame of reference is clearly challenging, but while the most irascible responses to such an outlook might tend to express disquiet at the perceived injustice being done to the victims of the past, to insist upon a victim's status as such is surely questionable and perhaps in and of itself indicative of trauma.[3] Genuine forgiveness may be so difficult to achieve precisely because of the substantive sense in which this act works to exonerate the other.

Freud (1923b) makes a distinction between repression and *Verleugnung* or "dis-avowal," a term he uses to signify the subject's refusal to consciously register a traumatic experience. Ferenczi and Rank (1923) suggest that while the major task of psycho-analysis is ostensibly the uncovering of the unconscious, the material that is most truly repressed "since it was never 'experienced' can never be 'remembered,' [so that] one must let it be produced on the ground of certain indications" (p. 31). Influenced by the work of Lacan and Bion, Davoine and Gaudilliere (2004) have expounded a theoretically challenging approach to intergenerational trauma that emphasizes the role of collective history. Working with their patients as "co-researchers," Davoine and Gaudilliere argue that all trauma is ultimately grounded in the collective concerns of history. Therapeutic work entails the effort to symbolize something that was not inscribed in the historical record. The reality of trauma persists in its remaining unmoved by the passage of time, and its facticity is in some sense jeopardized precisely when the traumatic reality of the unspeakable is rendered into words – only then can the event which was not yet registered as such be made subject to the possibility of being metabolized by history.[4] This approach appears to have parallels with Henrich's therapeutically suggestive notion of the *Denkraum*. Davoine and Gaudilliere contend that the past is alive to us in the present in so far as it remains as yet unspoken. Likewise, Henrich suggests that the intellectual past remains vitally accessible as a consequence of those paths of thinking that remain untrodden.

In emphasizing that reality consists only of the immediately given facts, the contemporary climate seems ever more opposed to the value of privacy; a theme which, as a consequence of the impingement of legislation on the conditions of confidentiality, becomes increasingly central within the context of therapy. With the emergence of the "information age" the manner in which the events of our lives have come to be recorded has grown incomprehensible – global information systems have developed to the extent that any item of data once registered as such might, even when erased at its source, still be reconstructed from untold locations elsewhere in the system. When the ritualistic burning of the past is no longer conceivable, we might recall the fear of soul-loss in respect to photography. Attending to the notion of change under observation, there appear to be clear resonances with the therapeutic setting. Might this suggest a relationship to the notion that analysands who are made subject to control studies demonstrate a greater likelihood of leaving treatment? In clinical work, the cautionary adage states: *if it's not documented, it didn't happen*. What, then, of the inverse proposition? Perhaps growing concern around the question of surveillance has a tendency to miss the point, at least in so far as the danger thus perceived is assumed merely to reside in the intentional misuse of data.

The metaphysician René Guénon describes a tendency nascent to the emergence of modernity that he terms the "solidification of reality" (Guénon, 2001, p. 115). Referencing Henri Bergson, who posits materiality as the domain of pure reason, Guénon argues that the world is locked into a state of materialistic decline wherein the techno-positivist worldview works its imaginal violence on the manifest (by making it more so) with oppressive efficiency. He writes:

> Much could be said about the prohibitions formulated in certain traditions against the taking of censuses otherwise than in exceptional cases, if it were to be stated that such operations, like all those of the "civil state" as it is called, have among other inconveniences that of contributing to the cutting down of the length of human life […] but the statement would simply not be believed; nevertheless, in some countries the most ignorant peasants know very well, as a fact of ordinary experience, that if the animals are counted too often far more of them die than if they are not counted; but in the eyes of moderns who call themselves "enlightened" such things cannot be anything but "superstitions."
>
> (p. 144)

If outside observation inhibits change, this suggests the necessity of the sealed therapeutic vessel. While in times past the magic circle was drawn to keep the spirits out, its function now is seemingly to keep them in. The question, then: how far are we willing to take William James's proposition that reality comprises beliefs reinforced by habits of action? Consider, as James did, that the scientific method as commonly understood is founded on a belief in a shared and objective reality governed by natural laws that can be discovered by means of observation and experiment. Much as in analysis, science searches for patterns, yet the intent is to establish a final model of truth that is globally coherent and endorsed by all. In distinction to the picture that might emerge if science were more widely fostered as a fundamentally creative endeavor, for economic reasons most scientific activity is in effect concerned with confirming a belief that what happened in the past will likewise hold good in the future. It is precisely by rendering a fixed history that this aim is realized. Hans Jonas (1966) refers to this tendency as an "ontology of death." Similarly, Baudrillard (1994) writes: "such is the vital function of the model in a system of death, or rather of anticipated resurrection, that no longer gives the event of death a chance" (p. 2). The scientistic pursuit of certainty seeks to confirm things as they are now assumed to be, as though residing in a perpetual condition of finalizing the details. Reflecting on the nature of psychosis, Bion (1962) remains skeptical:

> The breakdown in the patient's equipment for thinking leads to dominance by a mental life in which his universe is populated by inanimate objects. The inability of even the most advanced human beings to make use of their thoughts, because the capacity to think is rudimentary in all of us, means that the field for investigation, all investigation being ultimately scientific, is limited by human inadequacy, to those phenomena that have the characteristics of the inanimate. We assume that the psychotic limitation is due to an illness but that of the scientist is not. Investigation of the assumption illuminates disease on the one hand and scientific method on the other. It appears that our rudimentary equipment for "thinking" thoughts is adequate when the problems are associated with the inanimate, but not when the object for investigation is life itself. Confronted with the complexities of the human mind the analyst must be circumspect in following even accepted scientific method; its weakness may be closer to the weakness of psychotic thinking than superficial scrutiny would admit.
>
> (p. 282)

In attempting to accommodate the scientific perspective without treating lived experience reductively, developmental psychologist Daniel Stern (1985) makes a distinction between the "observed" infant and the "clinical" infant. The former is construed by developmentalists on the basis of behavior as exhibited by young children, while the latter is a psychoanalytic co-construction established jointly by therapist and adult analysand. Stern is attracted to the creative freedom implied by working with a subjective approach to therapy emphasizing the primacy of personal narrative (p. 15), but he moderates this view by suggesting that we should acknowledge that there are certain generalized developmental tendencies that can be discerned from working directly with the infant. In conducting his own observations, Stern videotaped very young children and exhaustively analyzed the recordings. With frame-by-frame attentiveness, he hoped to demarcate perceived commonalities and thus lay claim to the structurally fixed dimensions of self-formation.

As though caught between the scientific worldview's method of reality testing and a clear feeling for the primacy of narrative, Stern appears to recognize that the irreducibility of the subjective factor renders purportedly "objective" developmental schemas suspect (p. 17), yet this does not dissuade him from devising his own. He writes: "Evolution as it is daily encountered in the guise of 'human nature' acts as a conservative force in these matters, so that changing our general views of who infants are can change who they will become only to a certain degree" (Stern, 1985, p. 276). As though struggling in some respect for having conceded so much to scientific method, this passage occurs at the close of Stern's most influential work. Based on his direct experiences with the observed infant he concludes that individuals are constrained of necessity to a shared developmental schema, yet surely he moves beyond immediate experience in assuming that these shared tendencies are only subject to transformation in the course of biological evolution. The whole question of narrative potency rests precisely here, but in uncritically assuming the timeless and binding validity of a culturally prescribed narrative Stern has, in effect, already settled things. In distinction to the outlook offered in a participatory framework, there is a basic assumption being made that the power of narrative is only effective in so far as it can shape our skin-encapsulated[5] perspectives, but that an objective world beyond this remains unmoved. Against a position of this kind, philosopher and theologian Henri Corbin (1995) suggests:

> It is the cognitive function of the Imagination that permits the establishment of a rigorous analogical knowledge, escaping the dilemma of current rationalism which leaves only a choice between the two terms of banal dualism: either "matter" or "spirit," a dilemma that the "socialization" of consciousness resolves by substituting a choice that is no less fatal: either "history" or "myth."
>
> (p. 12)

The distinction Stern makes between the infant as a subject and the infant as an object of scientific inquiry only reinforces how inadequate our efforts must be in respect to drawing any final conclusions about the nature of the child's inner world. Infant research that would seek to do more than make rudimentary observations about the child's behaviors will inevitably come to express the particular prejudices of the researcher – the effort to legitimize our developmental thinking with recourse to the scientific study of babies comes to occlude the foundational role of subjectivity in any creative undertaking. The ideas a researcher propagates go unrecognized as bespeaking of basic commitments towards life that express the researcher's own character, and are passed off instead as proven and universally binding fact.[6]

Heidegger (1953/2000) cites Plato's *Republic* as the turning point in Western intellectual history, the juncture at which the verb *to be* is suppressed in preference for *being* as a noun. As the first instance in literature of the notion of a utopia, *The Republic* heralds a cultural movement that culminates in the process Guénon describes as solidifying. Martin Buber (1937), another figure greatly preoccupied with these issues, writes:

> In the It-world causality holds unlimited sway. Every event that is either perceivable by the senses and "physical" or discovered or found in intro-spection and "psychological" is considered of necessity caused and a cause. [...] Only those who know relation and who know of the presence of the You have the capacity for decision.
>
> (p. 100)

On the subject of cause and effect, Sri Nisargadatta Maharaj (1973) states:

> Causality is in the mind only; memory gives the illusion of continuity and repetitiveness creates the idea of causality. When things repeatedly happen together, we tend to see a causal link between them. It creates a mental habit, but a habit is not a necessity.
>
> (p. 58)

In what degree might a person's capacity to relate and be related to in an I–You situation be impaired by others relating to that same person as an It? Sri Nisargadatta Maharaj's contention that a habit is not a necessity leaves much room for inter-pretation. If we follow Guénon, then the prevalence of *it-ness* that he terms the "reign of quantity" suggests a process of spiritual decline with immediate ramification not simply for our lived experience, but for the very nature of the cosmic order. For such a thinker, the social construction of reality is no mere play of impressions, but the immediate expression of a corresponding spiritual situation. Guénon's radical critique of modernity rejects the notion of progress as conventionally understood, suggesting that the emergence of this very notion is itself indicative of decline. If there is some question of resisting this process, then it entails re-imagining history by means of a return to origins. Sri Nisargadatta Maharaj suggests that our mental habits are a function of the profane memory. Similarly, philosopher of consciousness Jean Gebser (1984) writes: "Memory is always time-bound; and what is even worse, it temporizes the timeless without transforming it into temporal freedom" (p. 324).

In light of these reflections, certain aspects of the undertaking to promote multiculturalism can start to seem like a particularly advanced form of the cultural imperialism that this movement would seek to challenge. Efforts to actively endorse plurality often have about them precisely the quality of a purportedly objective remembering that thinkers like Guénon and Gebser would have us reject. The widespread concern for celebrating cultural diversity might start to seem like a self-defeating project. To take one example, the predilection of contemporary anthropology for validating the wisdom of marginalized peoples – in so far as this project implies a process of documentation – threatens to result in the imaginal subjugation of the population in question. Wolfgang Giegerich (2007) has pointed to something similar in respect of environmental conservancy: "it is precisely by way of the protection of nature that its ontological annihilation is taking place" (p. 28). In formalizing and inscribing the beliefs of an indigenous culture, the "preservation of knowledge" might actually constitute an act of violence perpetrated against the people in question. This tendency is set in motion with the invention of writing and consequent erosion of the oral tradition, and comes to fruition with the rise of scientism coupled with the emergence of mass-literacy. If the recognition of non-Western practices is to amount to more than mere lip-service, the challenge thus reflected must be honored as such.

Drawing from World Health Organization studies which suggest that individuals diagnosed with schizophrenia are significantly more likely to recover in developing countries than in the West, Shulman (1997) observes that a person suffering with what Western medicine considers a psychopathological complaint are in other parts of the world more likely to be regarded as a "canary in the coal mine." In societies that are able to employ ritual to move freely between hierarchical and egalitarian structures of social organization, an individual's mental distress is more likely to be treated as a notice to the community that something needs to change. Crucially, this change is brought about by reintegrating the sick person into communal life by way of an adjustment in the community itself. In this fashion, the group can be said to function much like the human immune system (p. 71). The treatment of the mentally ill in this context serves the needs of the suffering individual, while in doing so protecting the wider community from deviating against nature. Where in a Western frame of reference it is generally assumed that the role of the clinician is to help change the patient, the perspective offered by Shulman suggests something quite opposite – that the patient's return to health is consequent upon having been able to bring about a change in the system itself. In keeping with such an outlook, it might be expected that any substantive response to present societal conditions will require a significantly more nuanced engagement with the claims of psychopathology.

Conflict and the future

> And since we are different, our help must be different.
>
> (Woolf, 1938, p. 143)

Few things seem more natural than the impulse to help. The history of psycho-therapeutic intervention, however, has witnessed a host of technical problems arising out of the effort to assuage human suffering. Additionally, clinicians have been challenged by critical engagement raising suspicion that the discipline of psychology serves largely as an administrative science, the role of which is to maintain existing power relations (Danziger, 1990). Drawing on Paulo Freire's concept of *concientización*,[7] liberation psychologist Ignacio Martín-Baró argues that the development of critical consciousness is essential if clinicians are to avoid normalizing individuals to the demands of a system which, when going unquestioned, comes to be considered natural. Psychology only meaningfully registers itself as a discipline in its own right when it promotes this notion of critical consciousness, the emergence of which is argued to be inherently transformative of the collective. Martín-Baró (1994) writes:

> The most serious problem of positivism is rooted precisely in its essence; that is, in its blindness towards the negative. Recognizing nothing beyond the given, it necessarily ignores everything prohibited by the existing reality; that is, everything that does not exist, but would, under other conditions, be historically possible.
>
> (p. 21)

While very much aware of the role social relations play in shaping subjectivity, the problem Martín-Baró perceives in the psychology of individualism is precisely the widespread tendency of reducing individuality to interpersonal relations – by emphasizing the role of the relational in forming the individual context, structural problems in society come to be perceived as personal problems that require the "help" of professionals. In a related sense, Frosh (1999) suggests that the practice of psychoanalysis is politically meaningful only in so far as it reflects an attempt to examine the relationship between collective influences and that which is most privately formative (p. 312).

Owing to the mandatory nature of the training analysis, psychoanalytic practice remains distinctive for its expectation that clinicians should extensively explore what motivates them to help others. Without a respectfully suspicious eye for these motivations and a theoretical approach that accommodates their relative unconsciousness, an obvious concern arises that the endeavor to help might result only in an unrecognized effort on behalf of the clinician to ameliorate his or her own position. This danger is liable to be most pressing when the helping party's motives strike them as most transparently reasonable. Thus, the psychiatrist who relies on pharmacology so as to control their own depression is liable to normalize this behavior by prescribing the same measure for others; the negative value of depression is taken as a given, and the possible ramifications of an attitude that would seek to immediately dispel this feeling remain unquestioned. Such an attitude seems to depend on an underlying philosophy wherein that which does not have an immediately apparent use value is assumed to be devoid of meaning – the importance of a given phenomenon is treated as though discernible in the terms of the system as it stands. That the symptom's persistence might inhere partly in the need that it be taken more seriously goes largely unconsidered.

The misappropriation of reason in service of an unquestioned rule of common sense is often most evident in the context of the cognitive-behavioral paradigm that has come to dominate mainstream psychotherapy. For the CBT practitioner, our unwanted thoughts and feelings are to be re-conceptualized so as to enable more adaptive ways of being in the world. Within this frame of reference, the individual is required to assert agency over the perceived problem and thus to restore order to their experience. Adaptation and health, it would seem, have come to be regarded as all but synonymous. But a pluralistic approach to psychotherapy cannot afford to emphasize ease of conformity as a basis for treatment.

The utopian ideal of normalcy has wide appeal, for it holds the promise of a final resting point for meaning. Equally, the anxiety often attending the creation of something new can be difficult to tolerate. One of the most obvious manifestations of the uncertainty of our times is reflected in the growth of fundamentalism – fundamentalists know what needs to be corrected. The rise of this tendency seems obviously undesirable, yet if the fundamentalist's position reflects a belief in having established the grounds from which the state of sickness can be determined, then there appears something rather ironic in jumping to regard the fundamentalist as sick. In keeping with this observation, the feminist psychoanalytic theorist Teresa de Lauretis (1994) suggests that the liberal emphasis on pluralism tends to affirm difference while asserting an underlying sameness that might itself be regarded as exclusionary (p. 5). Liberalism's relationship to fundamentalism suggests that in emphasizing the importance of dialogue, that which is in danger of falling unconscious is precisely the tendency to exclude. In preaching tolerance too keenly, we only give expression to our own lack of it.

With this recognition, one of the most hopeful things about the complex problems of the early twenty-first century may actually be our very inability to respond to them. Perhaps these challenges are not, as is frequently supposed, a call to action, but rather a call to self-reflection. The pressing economic and environmental crises of our age do not constitute an argument against introspective psychotherapy, but rather one in favor of it. Žižek (2007) speaks of "false activity":

> Even in much of today's progressive politics, the danger is not passivity but pseudo-activity, the urge to be active and to participate. [...] Those in power often prefer even a critical participation to silence – just to engage us in a dialogue, to make sure that our ominous passivity is broken. Against such an interpassive mode, in which we are active all the time to make sure that nothing will really change, the first truly critical step is to withdraw into passivity and to refuse to participate. This first step clears the ground for a true activity, for an act that will effectively change the coordinates of the scene.
>
> (pp. 26–27)

Žižek's endorsement of the refusal to participate is politically radical, yet quintessentially psychoanalytic. Clearly the notion of literally abstaining from action is non-sensical – one of the major claims of recent psychoanalytic thinking has in fact been to recognize the extent to which subjectivity is always shaping relationship. While this recognition has demonstrated that the classical supposition of neutrality is unsupportable when understood as such, affirming the power in silence equally reinforces the idea that change can be facilitated by adopting relatively passive modes of being in the world.[8] Considering the tremendous pressure exerted on clinicians to provide "solution-focused" treatments, we might have cause to be suspicious of any rhetoric that revels in promoting action (Summers, 2013a).

Notably, the major responses to positivist and post-positivist paradigms have themselves recapitulated the positivist concern with doing – critical theory, constructivist, *and* participatory approaches have all tended to measure the quality of their results on the basis of their capacity to stimulate action (Denzin & Lincoln, 2011, p. 101). Kohut (1959) writes:

> Perhaps the dread that causes the defensive neglect of the fact that introspection is such an important factor in psychoanalytic fact-finding is the fear of helplessness through tension increase. We are used to a continuous draining of tension through action, and are willing to accept thought only as an intermediary to activity, as a delayed action or trial action or planning.
>
> (pp. 465–466)

Even so, the psychodynamic commitment to refrain from offering solutions needn't require that we be unwilling to stand for the importance of assuming this very position. In keeping with such a notion, elsewhere Kohut (1971) stresses that the empathic attitude should not be maintained at cost to our intellectual integrity (p. 303). Psychoanalysis has an ethical obligation to guard its basic commitment to subjectivity, and not to satisfy itself in making accommodations to society in the name of professional survival – to do so only reinforces a sense that the profession has already folded.

In emphasizing the developmental role of accommodation to the environment as more determinative than innate endowment, relational thinking implies a fundamentally homeostatic model of the person as considered in relationship to their milieu – the political implications of this approach should be clear. Martín-Baró (1994) states:

> The homeostatic vision leads us to distrust everything that is change and disequilibrium, to think badly of all that represents rupture, conflict, and crisis. From this perspective, it becomes hard, more or less implicitly, for the disequilibrium in social struggle not to be interpreted as a form of personal disorder.
>
> (p. 23)

An emphasis on dialogue reflected in the ideal of striking a balance between opposing positions can threaten to become stifling. In the field at present, this is perhaps expressed most paradigmatically with the often cited acrimony as to whether psychoanalysis should be considered a science or a hermeneutic. In a certain sense this isn't so much a debate, as the sustained expression of precisely what the field has become. In failing to commit to a subjective ontology, psychodynamic discourse has lost its imagination (Adams, 2004) and become stuck. Only by adopting a properly psychological frame of reference does this impasse seem resolvable. Christou (1963) writes:

> Philosophy and natural science are under the pressure of a drive which impels them to expend their energies towards the solution of problems that exist only because of their dichotomy. Modern thought is characterized by its growing consciousness of the importance of discovering the unifying principle as well as by its realization of the logical impossibility of this principle being dis-covered within the framework of the established orders of philosophy and science as they stand at present. [...] since a unifying principle will have to say something about the world and also about the mind, the most likely place to find it will be the soul in so far as psychological reality seems to participate in both.
>
> (p. 30)

Martin Buber expresses something similar when he states: "Subjectivism is psy-chologization while objectivism is reification of God; one a false fixation, the other a false liberation; both departures from the way of actuality, both attempts to find a substitute for it" (Buber, 1937, p. 167). Thinking in terms of the participatory nature of the subject offers psychoanalytic practice an alternative to the reductions of both relativism and positivism – an approach wherein the individual's experience is considered primary.

In working with the foundational idea of an unconscious mind, psychodynamic thinking suggests that appearances are, to a greater or lesser extent, other than they seem. The trend signified by the emergence of this intellectual movement might therefore be encapsulated as a tendency to de-literalize. Where the field relies to an unnecessary degree on commonplace assumptions, the profession's cultural sig-nificance is in danger of being lost. This idiosyncratic movement in the history of ideas began life as a revolutionary practice, yet in the course of its development historical happenstance saw the field attain to an improbable degree of mainstream acceptance. That time has now passed. If the profession is to regroup and adjust to a more marginal role, it might benefit from returning to its subversive roots rather than seeking to anchor itself in social psychology. Such a return implies critical engagement with the mainstream and a willingness to question normative assumptions. Equally, the extent to which psychoanalytic discourse serves to affirm (or deny) biological reductionism is also the extent to which the field implicitly supports (or challenges) psychiatry in being able to continue basing its assumptions on ideological constructs which favor the financial interests of the pharmaceutical and insurance industries.[9]

Clinicians encounter the consequences of these pressures on a daily basis. If a significant aspect of the early work with patients falls within the scope of psycho-education, this task becomes ever more challenging the more deeply entrenched the culture of biological reductivism grows. While psycho-education in the context of a psychodynamic treatment seeks to empower the analysand to take their own experiences more seriously, objections to the legitimacy of "folk psychology" have precisely the opposite intention in expressing the idea that the average person is not sufficiently educated as to be able to fully appreciate the nullity of their own existence. A great many individuals seeking psychotherapy seemingly do so precisely as a consequence of not being able to attain a sense of agency and creative vitality, yet the present psychiatric paradigm only reinforces this. Clearly any form of substantive social change has as a prerequisite a basic sense of fascination with one's own experience, as opposed to a reliance on the assumed authority of others.

The manner in which public opinion comes to be shaped by debates concerning the nature of mind suggests a pressing responsibility for psychodynamic clinicians to speak out in defense of the field. Perhaps the most fitting response to the notion that psychoanalysis is self-indulgent is to insist upon drawing attention to the barely concealed misanthropy expressed in such a sentiment. Thinking in terms of "the unconscious" remains deeply significant as the basis for a nomenclature emphasizing the limits of reason and, by extension, offers the basis for an approach to the mind that is inherently pluralistic and respectful of the need for uncertainty. As Webster (2011) observes, since the unconscious cannot be mastered, our theoretical approaches must correspondingly renounce this notion of mastery (p. 10). While in recent years educated opinion has tended to concern itself with the threat of religious extremism, the rise of this tendency in the West may be directly correlated with the reductiveness of contemporary psychiatry, the nature of which has perhaps played a significant role in enabling the emergence of just such a climate: "If our experience is destroyed, our behavior will be destructive" (Laing, 1967, p. 28). With their carefully justified cynicism, eliminativists perceive in fundamentalist religion a distorted reflection of their own dogmatic literalism (e.g., Blackmore, 2007; Dennett, 2007; Dawkins, 2008). In the face of advancing neuroscience, for those following in the tradition of Ryle (1949) who would seek to refute the existence of mind itself, a claim is effectively made that the individual has no form of privileged access to the nature of their own personhood. When science attempts to secure this degree of authority for itself, we might ask how the mainstream intellectual community has come to give so much credence to these ideas in the first place.

Relational thinking has stressed that consciousness is a social phenomenon – this is reflected in the word's Latin root, *conscire*, meaning "to know together" or "to be mutually aware." Psychoanalysis, however, has from its inception been concerned to explore that which is *not* conscious. Considered etymologically therefore, the *un*-conscious refers to that which is *not* known together. To forge a link with something or someone implies a context against which this connection becomes appreciable. The restrictions of being an embodied person localized in time and space imply that we can only establish a limited number of significantly close relationships – not only with our environmental others but also, by extension, with our own otherness. The act of being born seems to entail choosing who we will be over and against those other selves we might have become otherwise, and the decision to enter life implies taking sides not only against others, but also against ourselves. Thus, we cannot help but affirm certain values – even when our intention is opposed to it. What seems essential in seeking to promote an atmosphere of relative tolerance is perhaps not the question of recognizing the other's values in ourselves so much as consciously engaging with how we relate to our own otherness. That is, diversity is not premised on merely contextualizing our truth claims, but on enduring the fundamental paradox that self-assertion entails a submission to becoming.

NOTES

Introduction

1 Founded by Stephen Mitchell in 1991, *Psychoanalytic Dialogues* is a leading peer-review journal devoted largely to relational thinking.

2 As explored later in the present work, objections to the fashion in which the Freudian emphasis on fantasy appears to draw away from the authentic existence of others may in fact be suggestive of limitations in how we theorize fantasy life rather than indicating the need to endorse a social psychology approach.

3 Greenberg and Mitchell (1983) establish a precedent for this approach in drawing attention to the ways in which neo-Freudians like Loewald and Kernberg might support their thesis.

4 By this designation Ringstrom primarily intends the work of Stolorow, Atwood, Orange, and Brandchaft. In keeping with Mitchell (1992) the present work treats the intersubjectivists as reasonably contextualized within the wider sweep of post-classical thinking generally designated in terms of a relational turn.

5 Consider Hoffman's (1998) statement: "Only *some* aspects of reality are socially constructed, in the sense that they are manufactured by human beings. Among those that are excluded is the fact that humans, *by their nature*, are active agents in the social construction of their worlds" (pp. 77, italics in original).

6 Taylor (2009) shows that the turn of the twentieth century witnessed a slew of psychodynamic theories, the historical role of which have since been obscured thus giving the impression that all lines of psychodynamic theorizing can be traced to Freud. This, Taylor argues, is not true: "The essential historical question is, why did psychoanalysis seem to take over so rapidly and so completely as to obscure this vibrant period that produced so many vibrant psychologies of the subconscious?" (p. 46). Jung and Adler, for example, have been widely portrayed as errant pupils of Freud's, where in actuality both had begun to form their own dynamic psychologies prior to involvement with the psychoanalytic movement.

Chapter 1: Clinical Intent

1 Psychologist and mental health rights activist Eleanor Longden (2013) speaks of the denial she encountered subsequent to her recovery from schizophrenia, with many professionals expressing such adamant faith in the psychiatric system that they argue the original diagnosis must by definition have been mistaken rather than acknowledge what would otherwise constitute a clear refutation of contemporary medical assumptions.

2 The authoritarian abuse of "resistance" as a concept can just as well be said to reflect the phenomenon itself (manifesting in the analyst) as indicating a need that this concept should be abandoned altogether (e.g., Schafer, 1992). Likewise, reframing this notion as merely expressing relational dynamics (Bromberg, 1995; Gerson, 1996) as opposed to potentially signaling a fear of the emergent unknown, while useful in encouraging the analyst to attend to their own role in shaping the clinical interaction, is at the same time potentially minimizing. An interpersonal reductivism of this kind can too readily reflect its own form of resistance, wherein the analyst seeks to have the patient collude in denying the fearfulness of the change in which they both participate by treating this shift as merely reflective of a re-configuration of present affairs.

3 The following argument was published by the author in an earlier form. See Brown (2015b).

4 Ironically, recent interest in the microbiome (Smith, 2015), while remaining within the sphere of biology and thus susceptible to the same kind of reductive treatment, may nevertheless offer some measure of support to this claim.

5 This is perhaps reminiscent of Mitchell's (2000) observation that we tend to confuse our minds with the way our bodies act as functional units in space (p. x). Altman (2007) has also expressed respect for the non-local view of consciousness, recognizing that the immediate dismissal of such a position is reflective of an unquestioned commitment to philosophical materialism. He is understandably concerned, however, that the transpersonal should not come to obscure the intersubjective. The participatory outlook reflected in the present work offers a direct response to this concern by demonstrating how a transpersonal perspective need not imply totalizing truth claims, and can accommodate a fundamental commitment to pluralism (see Chapter 3). For an extended argument from science in favor of the non-local view of consciousness, see Laszlo (2014).

6 Quoted in Conger (1927).

7 The consequence of a refusal to acknowledge this is also reflected in Mitchell's (1993) denial that temperament is a valid means of locating the core self since, as Mitchell justifiably observes, temperament doesn't lead to a particular formation of self without a context in which this can manifest (p. 128). While this observation as to the need of a social context is clearly valid, it remains to be shown why the role of social context should be *more* determinative than that of temperament.

8 Stepansky (2009) perhaps has such an approach in mind when he claims that theoretical pluralism results in an unproductive state of "truce" (p. 132), on which basis he argues for a solution in some respects similar to the one outlined by the early Stolorow and Atwood (1979) – he suggests that the field needs to align itself with a normative scientific paradigm by means of which objectively valid insights from the different theoretical camps might be brought into coherent relationship. Such a position however, fails to credit the extent to which conflict and paradox are creatively necessary. While Stepansky's concern for the lack of creative vitality that can be attendant to a disparate pluralistic discourse is well taken, the need suggested is surely for a more critically engaged plurality that can thrive on conflict, rather than a partial reconciliation conducted under the banner of totalizing truth claims.

9 It should be stressed that this needn't entail forgoing clinical language altogether, since such language will often authentically express something of the clinician's own feelings and ways of relating to the patient. Working in denial of the fashion in which clinical labels inform the clinician's experience of their patients would be every bit as counter-productive as failing to question the nature of these labels. It may even be argued that by representing the claims of the norm by way of pathologizing and a diagnosis the clinician in effect presents his or herself as the conduit for a change in the collective (see Coda).

Chapter 2: Rethinking the Psychoanalytic Subject

1 A related idea is offered by Kukla and Walmsley (2006) who observe that scientists often exhibit a methodological dualism in responding to the voluntarism–determinism debate; that is, they tend to work on the assumption that the world can be successfully

interpreted on the basis of a determined or probabilistic account, yet they adopt voluntaristic assumptions in the structure of scientific discourse. In the context of intellectual debate it is always assumed that a position can win favor through reasoned argument: "It's never claimed in a scientific paper that a view contrary to the author's was caused by the opponent's cultural milieu or by indigestion" (p. 20).

2   The equation of the mind with consciousness appears to deny the soul's perpetual activity and hence (potentially) its immortality. In this light, the religious significance of postulating the existence of an unconscious mind (or something equivalent) becomes clear.

3   A willingness to adopt these roles where clinically appropriate is of course essential. It cannot be sufficiently emphasized, however, that the therapeutic need thus reflected may be at least as much that of the analyst as it is that of the patient. Clinical receptivity is often most readily achieved when assuming a more parental role – a role that many patients no doubt benefit from falling into correspondence with. The danger thus presented, however, is in succumbing to an unconscious identification with these roles such as to avoid a more threatening encounter with the other.

4   This notion is adopted by Dennett (1991) in support of his efforts to refute "Cartesian materialism," as reflected in what he regards as the enduring tendency to imagine consciousness in terms of a theatre watched by a homunculus inside the brain.

5   While the overbearing constraints of academic specialism are well taken, paradigmatic boundaries develop partly out of the need for a pluralistic intellectual discourse. A far more profound tragedy would surely be implied in the existence of an academic milieu that lacked these fundamental conflicts. For a reflection on the importance of a more conscious relationship to the role of conflict in the development of a relationally focused pedagogy, see Brown (2016).

6   In the course of arguing for a participatory approach to inquiry, Heron and Reason (1997) suggest that constructivist approaches do not sufficiently account for the notion of experiential knowing: "that is, knowing by acquaintance, by meeting, and by felt participation in the presence of what is there" (p. 277). In emphasizing the role of experiential context, a participatory approach avoids the constructivist tendency of establishing truth only in community consensus: "Propositional truth is not only relative to the linguistic and conceptual context of the community in which it is uttered. It is also relative to the substrate of shared experiential primary meaning, which is the contextual ground for the use of language and conceptual exchange within the community" (p. 283).

7   Jung's psychology of relationship is sometimes misunderstood to rest upon a reductive notion of projection that fails to recognize the metaphysical implications of his conception of synchronicity (Brown, 2014b).

8   Needless to say, these conventionalized ways of speaking are not intended to reflect an essentialist commitment to fixed ideas concerning gender roles.

9   Samuels (2014) argues that the relational turn stems from the work of Carl Rogers, and suggests that this movement could reasonably be dubbed "humanistic psychoanalysis" (p. 184).

10 Henrich (1992) writes: "Any such work today in the problem domain of subjectivity, however, must also affect our endeavor to understand the philosophical movement that first made subjectivity the most important theme and even a principle of theory: the classical period of German philosophy" (p. 37).

11 For a reflection on the idea of a progression beyond progress in the context of the evolution of consciousness, see Brown (2013).

Chapter 3: Pluralism and Belief

1   This awkward yet very much necessary term is intended to broadly signify not only the transformative capacity of conventional religious practices, but also to embrace any question of change experienced in relationship to the felt sense of a living meaning. Smith et al., (2012) offer the following broad definition: "Spirituality is generally understood as the thoughts, feelings, and behaviors that an individual engages in search

of a relationship with the sacred or the transcendent. It can be understood as a search for that relationship or a process through which a person seeks to discover, hold on to, and even transform whatever it is he or she holds sacred" (p. 437).

2 In a related sense, transpersonalist Stanley Krippner opposed the creation of an APA division for transpersonal psychology precisely out of concern that the claims of the transpersonal would thus come to be minimized as a side issue rather than being understood as a fundamental challenge to the wider field (Schroll, et al., 2009, pp. 42–43).

3 Related to Levinas's approach to transcendence, Sherman (2008) argues that in its earliest stages participatory thinking emerged out of Plato's recognition that transcendence is necessary if we are to maintain an attitude of reverence for others (this thought is also reflected much later in the work of Nietzsche). Sherman suggests that Plato has often been misread as having sought to protect the realm of the divine from worldly contamination, where his concern was in fact to protect the value of the world by anchoring nature in the sacred.

4 In an earlier work, Orange (1995) herself states that the intersubjective approach she endorses values "the particularity of organized emotional experience and the *generality of humanness*" (p. 13, emphasis added).

5 This objection can be related to Kant's response to Baconian induction in the observation that passive representations without concepts are blind.

6 Passages occurring in this section have been revised from a previously published paper. Reprinted with permission and excerpted from original source: Brown, R.S. (2013). Beyond the evolutionary paradigm in consciousness studies. *The Journal of Transpersonal Psychology*, 45.2, 159–171.

7 Joseph Campbell's (1949) monomyth of the hero's journey offers perhaps one of the most well-known examples.

8 Jung (1952) writes: "I was driven to ask myself in all seriousness: 'What is the myth you are living?' I found no answer to this question, and had to admit I was not living a myth, or even in a myth, but rather in an uncertain cloud of theoretical possibilities which I was beginning to regard with increasing distrust. [...] So, in the most natural way, I took it upon myself to get to know 'my' myth, and I regarded this as the task of tasks" (pp. xxiv–xxv).

9 Jung himself confirms this connection, stating that the archetypes "are ideas *ante rem*, determinants of form, a kind of pre-existing ground-plan that gives the stuff of experience a specific configuration, so that we may speak of them, as Plato did, as *images*, as schemata, or as inherited functional possibilities which, nevertheless, exclude other possibilities or at any rate limit them to a very great extent" (Jung, 1921, para. 512).

10 A term adopted by Jung in reference to the non-psychic manifestation of the archetype in matter.

11 Ogden (1997) emphasizes speaking *from* the analyst's experience rather than *about* it. He states: "A direct statement of the metaphors that I have created in order to speak to myself about the experience of being with the patient is likely to rob the patient of an opportunity to create his own metaphors" (p. 729). In this light, Jung's approach to amplification may on occasion seem problematic from a technical point of view, even as the underlying intent remains valuable. For a sympathetic interpretation of Jung's notion of the Self considered in a Levinasean light, see Huskinson (2002).

12 Usually translated as "under erasure" – a textual practice originally developed by Heidegger and later adopted by Derrida. It consists of crossing a word through while retaining its legibility, in this way indicating both the term's inadequacy and its necessity.

13 As such, the approach to Jung's thinking being offered in the present context should be understood as an extrapolation from certain aspects of his psychology which may prove helpful in response to the epistemic shift in contemporary psychodynamic thinking.

14 Resonating with the relationship Jung proposes between the unknowable archetype per se, and the archetypal image, Bion (1961) speaks of proto-mental events that arise in the context of group psychology and manifest in one of three basic assumptions. Bion writes: "I cannot represent my view adequately without proposing *a concept that transcends experience*. Clinically, I make a psychological approach, and therefore note phenomena

only when they present themselves as psychological manifestations. Nevertheless, it is convenient to me to consider that the emotional state precedes the basic assumption and follows certain proto-mental phenomena of which it is an expression. Even this statement is objectionable because it establishes a more rigid order of cause and effect than I wish to subscribe to, for clinically it is useful to consider these events as *links in a circular series*" (p. 176, italics added).

15 This tendency clearly expresses an unwillingness to remain committed to a subjective ontology. Stephen Mitchell also struggled significantly with this question. Taub (2009) draws attention to how Mitchell turned away from thinking in terms of "human nature" owing to the incompatibility of this notion with postmodern thinking and the reliance such a notion seemingly has on biology, yet in his late work there are signs that Mitchell (2003) is explicitly falling back on biological thinking.

16 Within the Jungian community, recognition of this issue has sometimes been found wanting; perhaps because the question is readily conflated with matters arising around "individuation," and the ill-founded yet often encountered notion that this process is somehow inherent to the unconscious. The sense of a "process," however, is inevitably engendered by the meaning-making function of *conscious* experience. This is apparent where Jung (1945) writes: "If one believes that the unconscious always knows best, one can easily be betrayed into leaving the dreams to take the necessary decisions, and is then disappointed when the dreams become more and more trivial and meaningless. [...] The unconscious mind functions satisfactorily only when the conscious mind fulfills its tasks to the very limit" (para. 568). On a related note, Samuels (1985) draws attention to how the notion of the psyche as "self-regulating" has often led to a denial of tragedy.

17 In distinction to the outlook being offered in the present work, it should be noted that Lacan's anti-metaphysical sensibility is reflected most plainly in his assertion that there is no Other of the Other. Nevertheless, his ideas have often proven susceptible to a spiritually informed reading (e.g., Wyschogrod et al., 1989; Eigen, 1998; Pound, 2007). Defending Lacan against such interpretations, Žižek (2007) writes: "The virtual character of the big other means that the symbolic order is not a kind of spiritual substance existing independently of individuals, but something that is sustained by their continuous activity" (p. 11). It is worth noting, however, that from a participatory perspective a "spiritual substance" needn't be considered static nor independent of individuals.

18 The uroboros is a symbol depicting a serpent swallowing its own tail. Occurring in a range of religious and mythological traditions, this image is given particular importance in Jung's work as an alchemical image of renewal. Jung (1963b) writes: "In the age-old image of the Ouroboros lies the thought of devouring oneself and turning oneself into a circulatory process, for it was clear to the more astute alchemists that the *prima materia* of the art was man himself" (para. 513).

19 Rudolf Steiner (1924/2008): "Imagine that we actively bring the world of ideas into manifestation and, at the same time, realize that such manifestations are based on their own laws" (p. 36).

20 Skolimowski (1994) suggests: "Against the prevailing trend of empiricism, which has claimed: 'There is nothing in the mind that has not been previously in the senses,' participatory philosophy announces: 'There is nothing in the senses that has not been previously in the structure of our mind'" (p. xiii).

21 Quoted in Dews (1996).

22 Unsurprisingly, this position also comes to be reflected in a utopian politics, the pursuit of which requires the individual to submit the thrust of their own impulse to perfection in service to the social order.

23 It is noteworthy that Stolorow et al. (2002) make explicit reference to their widely endorsed conception of perspectival realism being related to this same parable (p. 121).

24 As von Franz (2001) memorably puts it: "The archetypes do not swim around in the collective unconscious like pieces of bread in a soup, but rather they are the whole soup at every point and therefore always appear in specific mixtures" (p. 9).

25 It might also be noted that the participatory approach to archetypal thinking being suggested in the present work also differs with the constructivist outlook offered by Young-Eisendrath and Hall (1991), who draw from Lakoff and Johnson's (1980) embodiment theory thus privileging the material world as constitutive of subjectivity and giving rise to the same kind of weak-form constructivism reflected in much relational theorizing.

Coda: Psychotherapy as a Catalyst for Collective Change

1 Reprinted with the permission of Hampton Press.
2 Passages appearing in this section of the text were published in an earlier form. See Brown (2015c).
3 For Judith Herman (1997), recovery from trauma ultimately depends on surrendering the sense of being special attendant to the status of a victim (p. 235). This idea might nevertheless need to be handled with caution (Brown, 2015a, p. 77).
4 On a related note, Jung's (2009) private conflicts are portrayed in *The Red Book* to extend beyond the personal sphere to reflect the problems of the dead. Jung's emphasis on grounding personal experience in the collective demonstrates the extent to which he, like Nietzsche, considered himself a physician of culture (Hillman & Shamdasani, 2013, p. 141). In the context of recent intergenerational trauma literature, the often mysterious nature of transmission seemingly supports Jung's idea of a transpersonal or collective unconscious. As Torok (1975/1994) states: "In general terms, the 'phantom' is a formation in the dynamic unconscious that is found there not because of the subject's own repression but on account *of a direct empathy with the unconscious or the rejected psychic matter of a parental objet.* Consequently, the phantom is not at all the product of the subject's self-creation by means of the interplay between repressions and introjections. The phantom is alien to the subject who harbors it" (p. 181, italics in original).
5 In addressing some of the ways in which Eastern thinking might challenge Western psychology, Alan Watts (2006) speaks of the "skin-encapsulated ego."
6 This is not to say that developmental theory is in no respect helpful, for to do so would itself entail dismissing the researcher's perception as "merely" subjective. The imaginative richness of developmental thinking indicates its usefulness in enabling us to explore suggestive new forms of creation mythology. Orange (1995) writes: "Developmental theories probably belong in psychoanalysis exactly to the extent that they further understanding, and they deserve exclusion or rethinking to the extent that they restrict of hamper it" (p. 27). The point at which these ideas become restrictive is surely in the degree to which they are portrayed as objectively valid. Consider, for example, Beebe's (2000, 2006) interest in the manner that the infant has been observed to periodically turn away from the caregiver's attention. While the moment of turning away is seemingly precipitated by an increase in the baby's heart rate (Field, 1981), the inference Beebe makes that the baby must have become "over-aroused" can only be speculative. The assumption being expressed is that the baby turns away from the caregiver because the infant is getting *too much* of something. This reflects an underlying sense that the thing of value is "out there," yet proves momentarily too rich to be digested. If, however, the value of the inner world and the baby's fantasy life were to be given theoretical priority, we might conjecture quite differently that the child's increased heart rate is a panic response arising precisely as a consequence of a *lack* of stimulation. Thus it seems wholly premature to ascribe the baby's behavior to a notion of over-arousal. It might be noted that this problem is directly related to the possibly fundamental question of whether dreams serve the needs of waking life, or waking life that of the dream (see Hillman, 1979).
7 Freire (1970) coins this term to denote a process by which individuals might overcome ideological constraints so as to interpret their worlds more creatively.
8 Such an outlook is reflected in the notion of "subtle activism." Building on the idea that consciousness is a non-local field in which individuals are embedded, subtle activism

explores the idea that social change can be effected indirectly through practices such as prayer and contemplation (Nicol, 2015).

9 It should be stressed that the neurological approach to consciousness needn't require this kind of reductionism. Popularizers like Sacks (1985) and Ramachandran (2011) – both of whom have been openly hospitable to psychoanalytic thinking – have emphasized the limits of neurology as an explanatory device for lived experience. That we might find support for psychodynamic thinking in reflecting on the nature of the brain is no doubt interesting, but it is surely worth stressing that support of this kind can equally well be found in world literature, current affairs, organized sports, the performing arts, advertising, or virtually any other domain of creative human endeavor. What seems inherently problematic in relating clinical work to conceptions of the brain is the implicit rejection of the metaphoric, thus registering the breakdown of our commitment to the subject – it is precisely the purportedly objective basis of brain science that holds such an immense attraction in "justifying" psychoanalytic causes.

REFERENCES

Adams, M.V. (2004). *The fantasy principle: Psychoanalysis of the imagination*. New York: Routledge.

Adler, A. (1938). *Social interest: A challenge to mankind*. Eastford, CT: Martino Fine Books.

Alexander, F.G., & Selesnick, S.T. (1966). *The history of psychiatry: An evaluation of psychiatric thought and practice from prehistoric times to the present*. New York: Harper & Row.

Altman, N. (2007). Integrating the transpersonal with the intersubjective: Commentary on Mary Tennes's "Beyond intersubjectivity." *Contemporary Psychoanalysis*, 43, 526–535.

Altman, N. & Davies, J.M. (2003). A plea for constructive dialogue. *Journal of American Psychoanalytic Association*, 51, 145–161.

Angell, M. (2000). Is academic medicine for sale? *New England Journal of Medicine*, 342, 1516–1518.

Aron, L. (1991). The analysand's experience of the analyst's subjectivity. In S.A. Mitchell, & L. Aron (Eds) *Relational psychoanalysis: The emergence of a tradition* (pp. 243–268). New York: Routledge.

——(1996). *A meeting of minds: Mutuality in psychoanalysis*. Hillsdale, NJ: Analytic Press.

——(2004). God's influence on my psychoanalytic vision and values. *Psychoanalytic Psychology*, 21, 442–451.

Aron, L., & Atlas, G. (2015). Generative enactment: Memories from the future. *Psychoanalytic Dialogues*, 25. 3, 309–324.

Aron, L., & Starr, K.E. (2012). *A psychotherapy for the people: Toward a progressive psychoanalysis*. New York: Routledge.

Atwood, G.E., & Stolorow, R.D. (2014). *Structures of subjectivity: Explorations in psychoanalytic phenomenology and contextualism* (2nd edition). New York: Routledge.

Barfield, O. (1988). *Saving the appearances: A study in idolatry*. Middletown, CT: Wesleyan University Press.

Barratt, B.B. (2013). *What is psychoanalysis? 100 years after Freud's "Secret Committee."* London & New York: Routledge.

Bateson, G. (1987). *Steps to an ecology of mind: Collected essays in anthropology, psychiatry, evolution, and epistemology*. Northvale, NJ & London: Jason Aronson.

Baudrillard, J. (1994). *Simulacra and simulation*. Ann Arbor, MI: University of Michigan Press.

Beebe, B. (2000). Coconstructing Mother–Infant Distress. *Psychoanalytic Inquiry*, 20, 421–440.

——(2006). Co-constructing mother–infant distress in face-to-face interactions: Contributions of microanalysis. *Infant Observation*, 9. 2, 151–164.

Benjamin, J. (1990). An outline of intersubjectivity. *Psychoanalytic Psychology*, 7, 33–46.

——(1995). *Like subjects, love objects: Essays on recognition and sexual difference*. New Haven & London: Yale University Press.

——(2010). Where's the gap and what's the difference? *Contemporary Psychoanalysis*, 46, 112–119.

Berdyaev, N. (1954). *The meaning of the creative act*. New York: Harper & Brothers.

Bertalanffy, L. (1968). *General systems theory*. New York, NY: George Braziller.

Bion, W.R. (1962). Learning from experience. In C. Mawson (Ed.) *The complete works of W.R. Bion* (Vol. 4, pp. 247–365). London: Karnac Books.

——(1970). *Attention and interpretation: A scientific approach to insight in psychoanalysis and groups*. In C. Mawson (Ed.) *The complete works of W.R. Bion* (Vol. 6, pp. 211–330). London: Karnac Books.

——(1961). *Experience in groups and other papers*. In C. Mawson (Ed.) *The complete works of W. R. Bion* (Vol. 6, pp. 95–257). London: Karnac Books.

——(1967). *Second thoughts: Selected papers on psycho-analysis*. In C. Mawson (Ed.) *The complete works of W.R. Bion* (Vol. 6, pp. 45–202). London: Karnac Books.

Blackmore, S. (2007). A dangerous delusion. Downloaded from: http://www.theguardian.com/commentisfree/2007/nov/13/adangerousdelusion

Blondel, M. (1893/1984). *Action* (O. Blanchette, Trans.). Notre Dame, IN: Notre Dame University Press.

Bohm, D. (1980). *Wholeness and the implicate order*. London: Routledge.

Bollas, C. (1987). *The shadow of the object: Psychoanalysis of the unthought known*. New York: Columbia University Press.

Boudry, M. & Buekens, F. (2011) The epistemic predicament of a pseudoscience: Social constructivism confronts Freudian psychoanalysis. *Theoria*, 77, 159–179.

Brandchaft, B. (2010). *Toward an emancipatory psychoanalysis: Brandchaft's intersubjective vision*. New York: Routledge.

Bromberg, P.M. (1995). Resistance, object-usage, and human relatedness. *Contemporary Psychoanalysis*, 31, 173–191.

——(1998). *Standing in the spaces: Essays on clinical process, trauma, and dissociation*. Hillsdale, NJ: Routledge.

Brooks, R.M. (2011). Un-thought out metaphysics in analytical psychology: a critique of Jung's epistemological basis for psychic reality. *Journal of Analytical Psychology*, 56. 4, 492–513.

——(2013). The ethical dimensions of life and analytic work through a Levinasian lens. *International Journal of Jungian Studies*, 5. 1, 81–99.

Brown, H. (2013). Looking for evidence that therapy works. *New York Times*, March 25, 2013 Retrieved from http://well.blogs.nytimes.com/2013/03/25/looking-for-evidence-that-therapy-works/

Brown, R.S. (2013). Beyond the evolutionary paradigm in consciousness studies. *The Journal of Transpersonal Psychology*, 45. 2, 159–171.

——(2014a). Affirming the contradiction: Jungian aesthetics, reification, and the shadow. *Jung Journal: Culture & Psyche*, 8. 3, 66–74.

——(2014b). Evolving attitudes. *International Journal of Jungian Studies*, 6. 3, 243–253.

——(2015a). An opening: Trauma and transcendence. *Psychosis: Psychological, Social and Integrative Approaches*, 7. 1, 72–80.

——(2015b). On the significance of psychodynamic discourse for the field of consciousness studies. *Consciousness: Ideas and Research for the Twenty First Century*, 1. 1, 1–12.

——(2015c). On the undisturbed functioning of memory. *Quadrant: The Journal of the C.G. Jung Foundation*, 45. 2, 59–68.

——(2016). Teaching disobedience: Jung, Montuori, and the pedagogical significance of conflict. *World Futures: The Journal of New Paradigm Research*, in publication.

Buber, M. (1937). *I and Thou* (R.G. Smith, Trans.). Edinburgh: T&T.

Campbell, J. (1949). *The hero with a thousand faces*. New York: Pantheon.

Carr, D. (1999). *The paradox of subjectivity: The self in the transcendental tradition*. New York: Oxford University Press.

Carus, C.G. (1846/1989). *Psyche: On the development of the soul* (R. Welch, Trans.). New York: Spring Publications.

Charles, M., & O'Loughlin, M. (2012). The complex subject of psychosis. *Psychoanalysis, Culture & Society*, 17, 410–421.

Cheetham, T. (2004). *Green man, earth angel: The prophetic tradition and the battle for the soul of the world*. Albany, NY: State University of New York Press.

Chessick, R.D. (2001). The contemporary failure of nerve and the crisis in psychoanalysis. *Journal of the American Academy for Psychoanalytic Dynamic Psychiatry*, 29, 659–678.

Chodorow, N. (1978). *The reproduction of mothering*. Berkeley, CA: University of California Press.

Christou, E. (1963). *The logos of the soul*. Vienna: Dunquin Press.

Combs, A. (2002). *The radiance of being*. St. Paul, MN: Paragon House.

Conger, G.P. (1927). Whitehead lecture notes: Seminary in logic: Logical and metaphysical problems. Manuscripts and Archives, New Haven, CT: Yale University Library.

Corbin, H. (1995). *Swedenborg and esoteric Islam*. (L. Fox, Trans.). West Chester, PA: Swedenborg Foundation Publishers.

Cranefield, P.F., & Federn, W. (1970). Paulus Zacchias on mental deficiency and on deafness. *Bulletin of the New York Academy of Medicine*, 46. 1, 3–21.

Danziger, K. (1990). *Constructing the subject: Historical origins of psychological research*. Cambridge, UK: Cambridge University Press.

Davies, J.M. (1996). Linking the "Pre-Analytic" with the Postclassical. *Contemporary Psychoanalysis*, 32. 4, 553–576.

Davoine, F., & Gaudilliere, J. (2004). *History beyond trauma*. New York: Other Press.

Dawkins, R. (2008). *The God delusion*. Boston, MA: Mariner Books.

de Lauretis, T. (1994). *The practice of love: Lesbian sexuality and perverse desire*. Bloomington, IN: Indiana University Press.

Dennett, D. (1991). *Consciousness explained*. New York: Back Bay Books.

——(2007). *Breaking the spell: Religion as a natural phenomenon*. New York: Penguin Books.

Denzin, N.K., & Lincoln, Y.S. (2011). *The SAGE Handbook of Qualitative Research* (4th edition). Thousand Oaks, CA: SAGE Publications.

Dews, P. (1996). *The limits of disenchantment: Essays on contemporary European philosophy*. London; New York: Verso.

Dolnick, E. (1998). *Madness on the couch: Blaming the victim in the heyday of psychoanalysis*. New York: Simon & Schuster.

Dunn, J. (1995). The intersubjective theoretical challenge to classical psychoanalysis. *International Journal of Psycho-Analysis*, 76, 357–374.

Eagle, M.N. (2003). The postmodern turn in psychoanalysis. *Psychoanalytic Psychology*, 20, 411–424.

——(2007). Psychoanalysis and its critics. *Psychoanalytic Psychology*, 24, 10–24.

Eigen, M. (1998). *The psychoanalytic mystic*. Binghamton, NY: ESF Publishers.

Ellenberger, H. F. (1958). A clinical introduction to psychiatric phenomenology and existential analysis. In R. May, E. Angel, & H.F. Ellenberger (Eds) *Existence: A new dimension in psychiatry and psychology* (pp. 92–126). New York: Basic Books.

Elliott, A. (2013). *Concepts of the self* (3rd edition). Oxford: Polity.

Fairfield, S. (2001). Analyzing multiplicity. *Psychoanalytic Dialogues*, 11, 221–251.

Ferenczi, S., & Rank, O. (1923). The development of psychoanalysis. In B. Wolstein (Ed.) *Essential papers on countertransference* (pp. 25–35). New York: New York University Press.

Ferrer, J.N. (2002). *Revisioning transpersonal theory: A participatory vision of human spirituality*. Albany, NY: State University of New York Press.

——(2008). Spiritual knowing as participatory enaction: As answer to the question of religious pluralism. In J.N. Ferrer & J.H. Sherman (Eds) *The participatory turn: Spirituality, mysticism, religious studies* (pp. 81–112). Albany, NY: State University of New York Press.

Ferrer, J.N., & Sherman, J.H. (2008). The participatory turn in spirituality, mysticism, and religious studies. In J.N. Ferrer & J.H. Sherman (Eds) *The participatory turn: Spirituality, mysticism, religious studies* (pp. 1–78). Albany, NY: State University of New York Press.

Ffytche, M. (2011). *The foundation of the unconscious: Schelling, Freud and the birth of the modern psyche*. Cambridge, UK: Cambridge University Press.

Fichte, J. (1982). *The science of knowledge* (P. Heath & J. Lachs, Eds & Trans.). Cambridge, UK: Cambridge University Press.

Field, T. (1981). Infant gaze aversion and heart rate during face-to-face interactions. *Infant Behavior and Development*. 4, 307–315.

Forrester, J. (1990). *The seductions of psychoanalysis: Freud, Lacan and Derrida*. Cambridge, UK: Cambridge University Press.

Foucault, M. (1961/2006). *History of Madness* (J. Murphy & J. Khalfa, Trans.). London & New York: Routledge.

——(1970). *The order of things: Archaeology of the human sciences*. London: Tavistock Publications.

Frank, M. (1989). *What is neostructuralism?* (S. Wilke & R. Gray, Trans.). Minneapolis, MN: University of Minnesota Press.

——(1995a). Is subjectivity a non-thing, and absurdity [unding]? On some difficulties in naturalistic reductions of self-consciousness. In K. Ameriks (Ed.) *The modern subject: Conceptions of the self in classical German philosophy* (pp. 177–198). Albany, NY: State University of New York Press.

——(1995b). Philosophical foundations of early romanticism. In K. Ameriks (Ed.) *The modern subject: Conceptions of the self in classical German philosophy* (pp. 65–86). Albany, NY: State University of New York Press.

——(1997). Subjectivity and individuality: Survey of a problem. In D.E. Klemm & G. Zoller (Eds) *Figuring the self: Subject, absolute, and others in classical German philosophy* (pp. 3–30). Albany, NY: State University of New York Press.

Freeman, A. (2003). *Consciousness: A guide to the debates*. Santa Barbara, CA: ABC Clio.

Freire, P. (1970). *Pedagogy of the oppressed*. New York: Continuum.

Freud, A. (1946). *The ego and the mechanisms of defense*. New York: International Universities Press.

Freud, S. (1900). *The interpretation of dreams*. In J. Strachey (Ed. & Trans.), *The standard edition of the complete psychological works of Sigmund Freud* (Vols 4 & 5, pp. ix–2013; 627). London: Hogarth Press.

——(1912). Recommendations to physicians practicing psycho-analysis. In J. Strachey (Ed. & Trans.) *The standard edition of the complete psychological works of Sigmund Freud* (Vol. 12, pp. 111–120). London: Hogarth Press.

——(1915a). Instincts and their vicissitudes. In J. Strachey (Ed. & Trans.) *The standard edition of the complete psychological works of Sigmund Freud* (Vol. 14, pp. 109–140). London: Hogarth Press.

——(1915b). Repression. In J. Strachey (Ed. & Trans.) *The standard edition of the complete psychological works of Sigmund Freud* (Vol. 14, pp. 141–158). London: Hogarth Press.

——(1923a). *The ego and the id*. In J. Strachey (Ed. & Trans.) *The standard edition of the complete psychological works of Sigmund Freud* (Vol. 19, pp. 12–66). London: Hogarth Press.

——(1923b). The infantile genital organization. In J. Strachey (Ed. & Trans.) *The standard edition of the complete psychological works of Sigmund Freud* (Vol. 19, pp. 141–148). London: Hogarth Press.

——(1923c). Two encyclopedia articles. In J. Strachey (Ed. & Trans.) *The standard edition of the complete psychological works of Sigmund Freud* (Vol. 18, pp. 235–259). London: Hogarth Press.

——(1926). *The question of lay analysis*. In J. Strachey (Ed. & Trans.), *The standard edition of the complete psychological works of Sigmund Freud* (Vol. 20, pp. 177–258). London: Hogarth Press.

——(1933). *New introductory lectures on psychoanalysis*. In J. Strachey (Ed. & Trans.) *The standard edition of the complete psychological works of Sigmund Freud* (Vol. 22). London: Hogarth Press.

Freundlieb, D. (2003). *Dieter Henrich and contemporary philosophy: The return to subjectivity*. Burlington, VT: Ashgate Publishing Ltd.

Frey-Rohn, L. (1974). *From Freud to Jung: A comparative study of the psychology of the unconscious*. New York: Putnam.

Frie, R. (2003). Introduction. In R. Frie (Ed.) *Understanding experience: Psychotherapy and postmodernism* (pp. 1–26). London & New York: Routledge.

Frie, R., & Reis, B. (2005). Intersubjectivity: From theory through practice. In J. Mills (Ed.) *Relational and intersubjective perspectives in psychoanalysis* (pp. 3–33). Lanham, MD: Jason Aronson.

Fromm-Reichmann, F. (1948). Notes on the development of treatment of schizophrenics by psychoanalytic psychotherapy. *Psychiatry*, 11. 3, 263–273.

Fromm, E. (1941). *Escape from freedom*. New York: Farrar & Rinehart.

Frosh, S. (1999). *The politics of psychoanalysis: An introduction to Freudian and post-Freudian theory (2nd edition)*. New York: NYU Press.

Gebser, J. (1984). *The ever-present origin*. Athens, OH: Ohio University Press.

Gerson, S. (1996). Neutrality, resistance, and self-disclosure in an intersubjective psychoanalysis. *Psychoanalytic Dialogues*, 6, 623–645.

Ghent, E. (1989). Credo – The dialectics of one-person and two-person psychologies. *Contemporary Psychoanalysis*, 25, 169–211.

——(1992). Foreword. In N.J. Skolnick & S.C. Warshaw (Eds) *Relational perspectives in psychoanalysis* (pp. xiii–xxii). Hillsdale, NJ: Analytic Press.

Giegerich, W. (1975). Ontogeny = phylogeny? A fundamental critique of E. Neumann's analytical psychology. In G. Mogenson (Ed.) *The neurosis of psychology: Primary papers towards a critical psychology* (pp. 19–39). New Orleans, LA: Spring Journal Books.

——(2007). Saving the nuclear bomb. In G. Mogenson (Ed.) *Technology and the soul: From the nuclear bomb to the world wide web* (Collected English Papers Vol. 2, pp. 25–36). New Orleans, LA: Spring Journal Books.

Gilligan, C. (1982). *In a different voice: Psychological theory and women's development*. Cambridge, MA: Harvard University Press.

Goethe, J.W. (1813/1949). Letter to Jacobi 6/1/1813. In H.J. Weigand (Ed. & Trans.) *Goethe: Wisdom and experience*. London: Routledge Kegan Paul.

Goodwyn, E.D. (2012). *The neurobiology of the gods: How brain physiology shapes the recurrent imagery of myth and dreams.* New York: Routledge.

Greenberg, J. (1991). *Oedipus and beyond: A clinical theory.* Cambridge, MA: Harvard University Press.

Greenberg, J.R. (1994). The changing paradigm of psychoanalysis. *International Forum of Psychoanalysis, 3,* 221–226.

Greenberg, J.R., & Mitchell, S.A. (1983). *Object relations in psychoanalytic theory.* Cambridge, MA: Harvard University Press.

Grof, S. (1992). *The holotropic mind: The three levels of human consciousness and how they shape our lives.* New York: HarperCollins.

Gross, Neil. (2006). Comment on Searle. *Anthropological Theory, 6.* 1, 45–56.

Grotstein, J.S. (2000). *Who is the dreamer, who dreams the dream?: A study of psychic presences.* Hillsdale, NJ: Routledge.

Guggenbuhl-Craig, A. (1980). *Eros on crutches: Reflections on amorality and psychopathy.* Irving, TX: Spring Publications.

Guénon, R. (2001). *The reign of quantity and the signs of the times.* Hillsdale, NY: Sophia Perennis.

Habermas, J. (1987). *The philosophical discourse of modernity: Twelve lectures.* Cambridge, MA: The MIT Press.

——(1994). *Postmetaphysical thinking: Philosophical essays* (W.M. Hohengarten Trans.). Cambridge, MA: The MIT Press.

Hacking, I. (1999). *The social construction of what?* Cambridge, MA: Harvard University Press.

Hadot, P. (2008). *The veil of Isis: An essay on the history of the idea of nature.* Cambridge, MA: Belknap Press.

Haraway, D. (1990). *Simians, cyborgs, & women.* New York: Other.

Harris, A. (1996). The conceptual power of multiplicity. *Contemporary Psychoanalysis, 32.* 4, 537–552.

Harris, A.E. (2011). The relational tradition: Landscape and canon. *Journal of American Psychoanalytic Association, 59,* 701–735.

Hartelius, G., & Ferrer, J.N. (2013). Transpersonal philosophy: The participatory turn. In H.L. Friedman & G. Hartelius (Eds) *The Wiley-Blackwell Handbook of Transpersonal Psychology.* New York: John Wiley & Sons.

Hartmann, H. (1939). Psycho-analysis and the concept of mental health. *International Journal of Psycho-Analysis, 20,* 308–321.

Hauke, C. (2000). *Jung and the postmodern: The interpretation of realities.* London; Philadelphia: Routledge.

Heidegger, M. (1927/1962). *Being and time.* (J. Macquarrie & E. Robinson, Trans.). New York: Harper & Row.

——(1947/1977). Letter on humanism. In *Basic writings* (pp. 213–265). New York: Harper & Row.

——(1953/2000). *Introduction to metaphysics.* New Haven, CT: Yale University Press.

Henrich, D. (1982). Fichte's original insight (D.R. Lachterman, Trans.). *Contemporary German Philosophy, 1,* 15–52.

——(1982). *Fluchtlinien.* Frankfurt am Main: Suhrkamp.

——(1987a). Philosophy and the conflict between tendencies of life. In *Konzepte: Essays zur Philosophie in der Zeit* (pp. 117–127). Frankfurt: Suhrkamp.

——(1987b). Was ist Metaphysik – was Moderne? Zwölf Thesen gegen Jürgen Habermas. In *Konzepte: Essays zur Philosophie in der Zeit* (pp. 11–50). Frankfurt: Suhrkamp.

——(1992). The origins of the theory of the subject. In A. Honneth, T. McCarthy, C. Offe, & A. Wellmer (Eds) *Philosophical interventions in the unfinished project of enlightenment* (pp. 29–87). Cambridge, MA: The MIT Press.

——(1997). *The course of remembrance and other essays on Hölderlin* (E. Förster, Ed.). Stanford, CA: Stanford University Press.

——(2003). *Between Kant and Hegel: Lectures on German idealism* (D.S. Pacini, Ed.). Cambridge, MA and London: Harvard University Press.

Herman, J. (1997). *Trauma and recovery.* New York: Basic Books.

Heron, J. (1996). *Co-operative inquiry: Research into the human condition.* London: Sage Publishing.

Heron, J., & Reason, P. (1997). A participatory inquiry paradigm. *Qualitative Inquiry, 3.* 3, 274–294.

Hillman, J. (1978). *The myth of analysis: Three essays in archetypal psychology.* New York: Harper Torchbooks.

——(1979). *The dream and the underworld.* New York: Harper & Row.

——(1983). *Archetypal psychology: A brief account.* Woodstock, CT: Spring Publications.

——(1995). A psyche the size of the Earth. In T. Roszak, M.E. Gomes, & A.D. Kanner (Eds) *Ecopsychology: Restoring the earth, healing the mind* (pp. xvii–xxiii). San Francisco: Sierra Club Books.

Hillman, J., & Shamdasani, S. (2013). *Lament of the dead: Psychology after Jung's Red Book.* New York: Norton.

Hoffman, I.Z. (1992). Reply to Orange. *Psychoanalytic Dialogues,* 2, 567–570.

——(1995). Oedipus and beyond: A clinical theory by Jay Greenberg. *Psychoanalytic Dialogues,* 5, 93–112.

——(1998). *Ritual and spontaneity in the psychoanalytic process: A dialectical-constructivist view.* Hillsdale, NJ: Analytic Press.

Hogenson, G. (2004). Archetypes: Emergence and the psyche's deep structure. In J. Cambray & L. Carter (Eds) *Analytical psychology: Contemporary perspectives in Jungian analysis* (pp. 32–55). New York: Routledge.

Horne, M.J. (2000) Philosophical assumptions in Freud, Jung and Bion: Questions of causality. *Journal of Analytical Psychology,* 45, 109–121.

Huskinson, L. (2002). The self as violent Other: The problem of defining the self. *Journal of Analytical Psychology,* 47, 437–458.

Jaspers, K. (1931/1957). *Man in the modern age* (E. Paul & C. Paul, Trans.). New York: Double Day Anchor Books.

Jodorowsky, A. (2010). *Psychomagic: The transformative power of shamanic psychotherapy.* Rochester, VT: Inner Traditions.

Jonas, H. (1966). *The phenomenon of life: Toward a philosophical biology.* New York: Harper & Row.

Jung, C.G. (1912/1916). *Psychology of the unconscious: A study of the transformations and symbolisms of the libido* (B.M. Hinkle, Trans.). New York: Moffat, Yard and Company.

——(1919). Instinct and the unconscious. In G. Adler & R.F.C. Hull (Eds & Trans.) *The collected works of C.G. Jung* (Vol. 8, pp. 129–138). Princeton, NJ: Princeton University Press.

——(1921). *Psychological types.* In G. Adler & R.F.C. Hull (Eds & Trans.) *The collected works of C.G. Jung* (Vol. 6). Princeton, NJ: Princeton University Press.

——(1928). The relations between the ego and the unconscious. In G. Adler & R.F.C. Hull (Eds & Trans.) *The collected works of C.G. Jung* (Vol. 7, pp. 121–292). Princeton, NJ: Princeton University Press.

——(1935). The Tavistock lectures. In G. Adler & R.F.C. Hull (Eds & Trans.) *The collected works of C.G. Jung* (Vol. 18, pp. 1–182). Princeton, NJ: Princeton University Press.

——(1939). Psychological commentary on "The Tibetan book of the great libera- tion." In G. Adler & R.F.C. Hull (Eds & Trans.) *The collected works of C.G. Jung* (Vol. 11, pp. 475–508). Princeton, NJ: Princeton University Press.

——(1945). On the nature of dreams. In G. Adler & R.F.C. Hull (Eds & Trans.) *The collected works of C.G. Jung* (Vol. 8, pp. 281–297). Princeton, NJ: Princeton University Press.

——(1947). On the nature of the psyche. In G. Adler & R.F.C. Hull (Eds & Trans.) *The collected works of C.G. Jung* (Vol. 8, pp. 159–236). Princeton, NJ: Princeton University Press.

——(1950). *Aion: Researches into the phenomenology of the self.* In G. Adler & R.F.C. Hull (Eds & Trans.) *The collected works of C.G. Jung* (Vol. 9ii). Princeton, NJ: Princeton University Press.

——(1951). The psychology of the child archetype. In G. Adler & R.F.C. Hull (Eds & Trans.) *The collected works of C.G. Jung* (Vol. 9i, pp. 151–181). Princeton, NJ: Princeton University Press.

——(1952). *Symbols of transformation: An analysis of the prelude to a case of schizophrenia.* In G. Adler & R.F.C. Hull (Eds & Trans.) *The collected works of C.G. Jung* (Vol. 5). Princeton, NJ: Princeton University Press.

——(1954a). *Answer to Job.* In G. Adler & R.F.C. Hull (Eds & Trans.) *The collected works of C.G. Jung* (Vol. 11, pp. 355–470). Princeton, NJ: Princeton University Press.

——(1954b). Archetypes of the collective unconscious. In G. Adler & R.F.C. Hull (Eds & Trans.) *The collected works of C.G. Jung* (Vol. 9i, pp. 3–41). Princeton, NJ: Princeton University Press.

——(1958). The transcendent function. In G. Adler & R.F.C. Hull (Eds & Trans.) *The collected works of C.G. Jung* (Vol. 8, pp. 67–91). Princeton, NJ: Princeton University Press.

——(1959). Flying saucers: A modern myth of things seen in the skies. In G. Adler & R.F. C. Hull (Eds & Trans.) *The collected works of C.G. Jung* (Vol. 10, pp. 307–433). Princeton, NJ: Princeton University Press.

——(1963a). *Memories, dreams, reflections* (R. Winston & C. Winston, Trans., A. Jaffe, Ed.). New York: Pantheon Books.

——(1963b). *Mysterium coniunctionis: An inquiry into the separation and synthesis of psychic opposites in alchemy.* In G. Adler & R.F.C. Hull (Eds & Trans.) *The collected works of C.G. Jung* (Vol. 14). Princeton, NJ: Princeton University Press.

——(1964). *Man and his symbols.* New York: Doubleday.

——(2009). *The red book: Liber novus.* New York: W.W. Norton & Company.

Kanner, L. (1949). Problems of nosology and psychodynamics in early childhood autism. *American Journal of Orthopsychiatry,* 19. 3, 416–426.

Kant, I. (1787/1998). *Critique of pure reason* (P. Guyer & A.W. Wood, Eds. & Trans.). New York: Cambridge University Press.

Kegan, R. (1982). *The evolving self: Problem and process in human development.* Cambridge, MA: Harvard University Press.

——(1994). *In over our heads: The mental demands of modern life.* Cambridge, MA: Harvard University Press.

Kohut, H. (1959). Introspection, empathy, and psychoanalysis – An examination of the relationship between mode of observation and theory. *Journal of the American Psychoanalytic Association,* 7, 459–483.

——(1971). *The analysis of the self: A systematic approach to the psychoanalytic treatment of narcissistic personality disorders.* London: International Universities Press.

——(1977). *The restoration of the self.* New York: International Universities Press.

Koyré, A. (1968). *Metaphysics and Measurement*. Cambridge, MA: Harvard University Press.

Kuhn, T. (1970). *The structure of scientific revolutions* (2nd edition). Chicago: Chicago University Press.

Kukla, A. (2000). *Social constructivism and the philosophy of science*. London & New York: Routledge.

Kukla, A., & Walmsley, J. (2006). *Mind: A historical & philosophical introduction to the major theories*. Indianapolis, IN: Hackett Publishing Company.

Lacan, J. (1954–55/1991). *The seminar of Jacques Lacan: The ego in Freud's theory and in the technique of psychoanalysis, 1954–1955* (J.A. Miller, Ed. & S. Tomaselli, Trans.). New York: Norton.

——(1959–60/1997). *The seminar of Jacques Lacan: The ethics of psychoanalysis, 1959–1960* (J.A. Miller, Ed. & D. Porter, Trans.). New York: Norton.

——(1966/2005). *Écrits: A selection* (B. Fink, Ed. & Trans.). New York: Norton.

Laing, R.D. (1967). *The politics of experience*. New York: Pantheon Books.

Lakatos, I. (1970). Science: Reason or religion. In I. Lakatos & A. Musgrave (Eds) *Criticism and the growth of knowledge*. Cambridge, UK: Cambridge University Press.

Lakoff, G., & Johnson, M. (1980). *Metaphors we live by*. Chicago: University of Chicago Press.

Langs, R. (1993). Psychoanalysis: Narrative myth or narrative science. *Contemporary Psychoanalysis*, 29, 555–594.

Laszlo, I. (2014). *The immortal mind: Science and the continuity of consciousness beyond the brain*. Rochester, NY: Inner Traditions.

Latour, B., & Woolgar, S. (1986). *Laboratory life: The social construction of scientific facts* (2nd edition). Princeton, NJ: Princeton University Press.

Levenson, E. (1972). *The fallacy of understanding*. New York: Basic Books.

——(1992). Mistakes, errors, and oversights. *Contemporary Psychoanalysis*, 28, 555–571.

——(1961/1969). *Totality and infinity* (A. Lingis, Trans.). Pittsburgh, PA: Duquesne University Press.

——(1962/1997). Transcendence and height. In A.T. Peperzak, S. Critchley, & R. Bernasconi (Eds) *Emmanuel Levinas: Basic philosophical writings* (pp. 11–32). Bloomington, IN: Indiana University Press.

——(1984/1997). Transcendence and intelligibility. In A.T. Peperzak, S. Critchley, & R. Bernasconi (Eds) *Emmanuel Levinas: Basic philosophical writings* (pp. 149–160). Bloomington, IN: Indiana University Press.

——(1999). *Alterity and transcendence*. New York: Columbia University Press.

Loewald, H.W. (1980). *Papers on psychoanalysis*. New Haven, CT: Yale University Press.

——(2000). *The essential Loewald: Collected papers and monographs*. Hagerstown, MD: University Publishing Group.

Longden, E. (2013). Eleanor Longden: The voices in my head [Video file]. Retrieved from http://www.ted.com/talks/eleanor_longden_the_voices_in_my_head?language=en

Lotterman, A. (2015). *Psychotherapy for people diagnosed with schizophrenia: Specific techniques*. New York: Routledge.

MacLennan, B.J. (2006). Evolutionary Jungian psychology. *Psychological Perspectives*, 49, 9–28.

Makari, G. (2008). *Revolution in mind: The creation of psychoanalysis*. New York: Harper Perennial.

Mann, T. (1937). *Freud, Goethe, Wagner*. New York: Alfred A. Knopf.

Marlan, S. (2005). *The black sun: The alchemy and art of darkness*. College Station, TX: Texas A&M University Press.

Martìn-Baró, I. (1994). *Writings for a liberation psychology*. Cambridge, MA: Harvard University Press.

Maslow, A. (1970). *Motivation and personality* (2nd edition). New York: Harper & Row.

Masson, J. M. (1984). *Assault on truth: Freud's suppression of the seduction theory.* New York: Farrar, Straus & Giroux.

May, R. (1958a). The origins and significance of the existential movement in psychology. In R. May, E. Angel, & H.F. Ellenberger (Eds) *Existence: A new dimension in psychiatry and psychology* (pp. 3–36). New York: Basic Books.

——(1958b). Contributions of existential psychotherapy. In R. May, E. Angel, & H.F. Ellenberger (Eds) *Existence: A new dimension in psychiatry and psychology* (pp. 37–91). New York: Basic Books.

McFadden, J. (2012). Dissociation re-enters psychoanalysis – Janet and Jung must be smiling on the balcony: a reviewer's comment. *Journal of Analytical Psychology,* 57. 5, 682–683.

McGrath, S.J. (2012). *The dark ground of spirit: Schelling and the unconscious.* New York: Routledge.

Mead, G.H. (1964). *George Herbert Mead: On social psychology.* (A. Strauss, Ed.). Chicago: University of Chicago Press.

Mensch, J.R. (1988). *Intersubjectivity and transcendental idealism.* Albany, NY: SUNY Press.

Miller, J.C. (2004). *The transcendent function: Jung's model of psychological growth through dialogue with the unconscious.* Albany, NY: State University of New York Press.

Mills, J. (2005). Process psychology. In J. Mills (Ed.) *Relational and intersubjective perspectives in psychoanalysis* (pp. 279–308). Lanham, MD: Jason Aronson.

——(2012). *Conundrums: A critique of contemporary psychoanalysis.* New York: Routledge.

——(2013). Jung's metaphysics. *International Journal of Jungian Studies,* 5. 1, 19–43.

——(2014). *Underworlds: Philosophies of the unconscious from psychoanalysis to metaphysics.* Hove: Routledge.

Mitchell, S.A. (1992). Commentary on Trop and Stolorow's "Defense analysis in self psychology." *Psychoanalytic Dialogues,* 2, 443–453.

——(1993). *Hope and dread in psychoanalysis.* New York: Basic Books.

——(1997). *Influence and autonomy in psychoanalysis.* Hillsdale, NJ: Analytic Press.

——(2000). *Relationality: From attachment to intersubjectivity.* New York: Routledge.

——(2003). *Can love last? The fate of romance over time.* New York: Norton.

Mitchell, S.A., & Aron, L. (1999). Preface. In S.A. Mitchell & L. Aron (Eds) *Relational psychoanalysis: The emergence of a tradition* (pp. ix–xx). New York: Routledge.

Mitchell, S.A., & Harris, A. (2004). What's American about American psychoanalysis? *Psychoanalytic Dialogues,* 14, 165–191.

Modell, A.H. (1991). The therapeutic relationship as a paradoxical experience. *Psychoanalytic Dialogues,* 1, 13–28.

Moran, F. (1993). *Subject and agency in psychoanalysis: Which is to be master?* New York: NYU Press.

Morin, E. (1999). *Homeland earth: A manifesto for the new millennium* (S.M. Kelly & R. LaPointe, Trans.). New York: Hampton Press.

——(2008). *On complexity* (R. Postel, Trans.). New York: Hampton Press.

Morton, T. (2007) *Ecology without nature: Rethinking environmental aesthetics.* Cambridge, MA: Harvard University Press.

Nagel, T. (1986). *The view from nowhere.* New York: Oxford University Press.

Nagl, L. (1988). Zeigt dis Habermassche kommunikationstheorie einen "ausweg aus der subjekt- philosophie"? Erwägungen zur studie "der philosophische diskurs der moderne." In M. Frank, G. Raulet, and W. Van Reijen (Eds) *Die Frage nach dem Subjekt.* Frankfurt am Main: Suhrkamp.

Needleman, J. (1975). *A sense of the cosmos: The encounter of modern science and ancient truth.* Garden City, NY: Doubleday.

Neumann, E. (1954). *The origin and history of consciousness*. Princeton, NJ: Princeton University Press.

Nicholls, A., & Liebscher, M. (Eds). (2012). *Thinking the unconscious: Nineteenth-century German thought*. Cambridge, UK: Cambridge University Press.

Nicol, D. (2015). *Subtle activism: The inner dimension of social and planetary transformation*. Albany, NY: SUNY Press.

Nietzsche, F. (1881/1997). *Daybreak: Thoughts on the prejudices of morality* (M. Clark & B. Leiter, Eds). Cambridge, UK: Cambridge University Press.

——(1886/1992). *The birth of tragedy*. In W. Kaufman (Ed. & Trans.) *Basic writings of Nietzsche* (pp. 1–144). New York: The Modern Library.

——(1888/1992). *The case of Wagner*. In W. Kaufman (Ed. & Trans.) *Basic writings of Nietzsche* (pp. 601–654). New York: The Modern Library.

Nisargadatta (1973). *I am that*. Mumbai: Chetana.

Nissim-Sabat, M. (2005). Where do we go from here. In J. Mills (Ed.) *Relational and intersubjective perspectives in psychoanalysis* (pp. 201–222). Lanham MD: Jason Aronson.

Ogden, T.H. (1997). Reverie and metaphor. *International Journal of Psycho-Analysis*, 78, 719–732.

——(1977). *Subjects of analysis*. Northvale, NJ: Jason Aronson.

——(1997). *Reverie and interpretation*. Northvale, NJ: Jason Aronson.

Orange, D.M. (1992). Perspectival realism and social constructivism: Commentary on Irwin Hoffman's "Discussion: Toward a social-constructivist view of the psychoanalytic situation." *Psychoanalytic Dialogues*, 2, 561–565.

——(1995). *Emotional understanding: Studies in psychoanalytic epistemology*. New York: The Guilford Press.

——(2003). Why language matters to psychoanalysis. *Psychoanalytic Dialogues*, 13, 77–103.

——(2009). *Thinking for clinicians: Philosophical resources for contemporary psychoanalysis and the humanistic psychotherapies*. New York: Routledge.

——(2011). *The suffering stranger: Hermeneutics for everyday clinical practice*. New York, NY: Routledge.

Pine, F. (1990). *Drive, ego, object, & self*. New York, NY: Basic Books.

——(1998). *Diversity and direction in psychoanalytic technique*. New Haven, CT: Yale University.

Pinkard, T. (2002). *German philosophy 1760–1860: The legacy of idealism*. Cambridge, UK: Cambridge University Press.

Pound, M. (2007). *Theology, psychoanalysis and trauma*. London: SCM Press.

Purcell, M. (2003) Notes and comments: "Levinas and theology"? The scope and limits of doing theology with Levinas. *Heythrop Journal*, 44, 468–479.

Ramachandran, V.S. (2011). *The tell-tale brain: A neuroscientist's quest for what makes us human*. New York: Norton.

Rank, O. (1936). *Truth and reality: A life history of the human will*. New York: Alfred A. Knopf.

Rapaport, D. (1957). The theory of ego autonomy: A generalization. In M. Gill (Ed.) *The collected papers of David Rapaport* (pp. 722–744). New York: Basic Books.

Renik, O. (2006). *Practical psychoanalysis*. New York: Other Press.

Rensma, R. (2013). Analytical psychology and the ghost of Lamarck: Did Jung believe in the inheritance of acquired characteristics? *Journal of Analytical Psychology*, 58, 258–277.

Richards, A.D. (2003). Psychoanalytic discourse at the turn of our century: A plea for a measure of humility. *Journal of the American Psychoanalytic Association*, 51, 73–89.

Ricoeur, P. (1970). *Freud and philosophy: An essay on interpretation.* New Haven, CT & London: Yale University Press.

——(1986). The self in psychoanalysis and in phenomenological philosophy. *Psychoanalytic Inquiry*, 6, 437–458.

Ringstrom, P.A. (2010). Meeting Mitchell's challenge: A comparison of relational psychoanalysis and intersubjective systems theory. *Psychoanalytic Dialogues*, 20, 196–218.

Rosenbaum, R. (2012). Psychoanalysis, psi phenomena, and spiritual space: Common ground. In L.J. Miller (Ed.) *The Oxford handbook of psychology and spirituality* (pp. 271–285). New York: Oxford University Press.

Ryle, G. (1949). *The concept of mind.* Chicago: University of Chicago Press.

Sacks, O. (1985). *The man who mistook his wife for a hat and other clinical tales.* New York: Summit Books.

Samuels, A. (1985). *Jung and the post-Jungians.* London: Routledge & Kegan Paul.

——(2014). Shadows of the therapy relationship. In D. Loewenthal & A. Samuels (Eds) *Relational psychotherapy, psychoanalysis and counseling: Appraisals and reappraisals* (pp. 184–192). London & New York: Routledge.

Schafer, R. (1992) *Retelling a life.* New York: Basic Books.

Schelling, F.W.J. (1799/2004). *First outline of a system of the philosophy of nature* (K.R. Peterson, Trans.). Albany, NY: SUNY Press.

——(1800/1993). *System of transcendental idealism (1800).* Charlottesville, VA: University of Virginia Press.

——(1813/1997). *Ages of the world* (S. Žižek, Ed., J. Norman, Trans.). Ann Arbor, MI: University of Michigan Press.

Schroll, M.A., Krippner, S., Vich, M., Fadiman, J., & Mojeiko, V. (2009). Reflections on transpersonal psychology's 40th anniversary, ecopsychology, transpersonal science, and psychedelics: A conversation forum. *International Journal of Transpersonal Studies*, 28, 39–52.

Schwartz-Salant, N. (1986). *Narcissism and character transformation: The psychology of narcissistic character disorders.* Toronto: Inner City Books.

Scott, D. (2014). *Gilbert Simondon's psychic and collective individuation: A critical introduction and guide.* Edinburgh: Edinburgh University Press.

Searle, J.R. (1994). *The rediscovery of the mind.* Cambridge MA: MIT Press.

——(1998). *The construction of social reality.* Florence, MA: Free Press.

——(2002). Why I am not a property dualist. *Journal of Consciousness Studies*, 9. 12, 57–64.

Seidel, G. (2010). From idealism to romanticism and Leibniz' logic. In D. Breazeale & T. Rockmore (Eds) *Fichte, German idealism, and early romanticism* (pp. 179–188). New York: Rodopi.

Seigel, J. (2005). *The idea of the self: Thought and experience in Western Europe since the Seventeenth Century.* New York: Cambridge University Press.

Shamdasani, S. (2004). *Jung and the making of modern psychology: The dream of a science.* Cambridge, UK: Cambridge University Press.

——(2012). *C.G. Jung: A biography in books.* New York: Norton.

Sherman, J.H. (2008). A genealogy of participation. In J.N. Ferrer & J.H. Sherman (Eds) *The participatory turn: Spirituality, mysticism, religious studies* (pp. 81–112). Albany, NY: State University of New York Press.

Shulman, H. (1997). *Living at the edge of chaos: Complex systems in culture and psyche.* Einsiedeln: Daimon Verlag.

Skolimowski, H. (1994). *The participatory mind: A new theory of knowledge and of the universe.* New York & London: Penguin.

Slavin, M.O. (2001). Constructivism with a human face. *Psychoanalytic Dialogues*, 11, 405–429.

Smith, B.W., Ortiz, J.A., Wiggins, K.T., Bernard, J.F., & Dalen, J. (2012). Spirituality, resilience, and positive emotions. In *The Oxford handbook of psychology and spirituality* (L.J. Miller, Ed.). New York: Oxford University Press.

Smith, P.A. (2015). Gut feelings. *New York Times*, June 23, p. MM46.

Sorenson, R.L. (2004). *Minding spirituality*. New York: Routledge.

Spezzano, C. (1996a). The three faces of two-person psychology: Development, ontology, and epistemology. *Psychoanalytic Dialogues*, 6, 599–622.

Spezzano, C. (1996b). Toward an intrapsychic-intersubjective dialectic: Reply to commentary. *Psychoanalytic Dialogues*, 6, 675–688.

——(1998) Listening and interpreting – How relational analysts kill time between disclosures and enactments: Commentary on papers by Bromberg and by Greenberg. *Psychoanalytic Dialogues*, 8, 237–246.

Steiner, R. (1924/2008). *Goethe's theory of knowledge: An outline of the epistemology of his worldview* (P. Clemm, Trans.). Great Barrington, MA: SteinerBooks.

Stepansky, P.E. (2009). *Psychoanalysis at the margins*. New York: Other Press.

Sterba, R. (1934). The fate of the ego in analytic therapy. *International Journal of Psycho-Analysis*, 15, 117–126.

Stern, D. (1985). *The interpersonal world of the infant: A view from psychoanalysis and developmental psychology*. New York: Basic Books.

Stern, D.B. (1991). A philosophy for the embedded analyst – Gadamer's hermeneutics and the social paradigm of psychoanalysis. *Contemporary Psychoanalysis*, 27, 51–80.

——(1997). *Unformulated experience: From dissociation to imagination in psychoanalysis*. New York: Routledge.

——(2009). Curiosity. *Contemporary Psychoanalysis*, 45, 292–305.

Stevens, A. (1982). *Archetypes*. New York: William Morrow.

Stolorow, R.D. (2003). On the impossibility of immaculate perception – There is no relationship without interpretation, and there is no interpretation without relationship. *Progress in Self Psychology*, 19, 217–223.

——(2011). *World, affectivity, trauma: Heidegger and post-Cartesian psychoanalysis*. New York: Routledge.

Stolorow, R.D., & Atwood, G.E. (1979). *Faces in a cloud: Subjectivity in personality theory*. Northvale, NJ: Jason Aronson.

——(1992). *Contexts of being: The intersubjective foundations of psychological life*. Hillsdale, NJ: Analytic Press.

Stolorow, R.D., Atwood, G.E., & Orange, D.M. (2002). *Worlds of experience interweaving philosophical and clinical dimensions in psychoanalysis*. New York: Basic Books.

Strauss, L. (1989) Progress or return? In H. Gildin (Ed.) *An introduction to political philosophy: Ten essays* (pp. 282–283). Detroit, MI: Wayne State University Press.

Sullivan, H.S. (1940). Conceptions of modern psychiatry. *Psychiatry*, 3, 35–45.

——(1950). The illusion of personal individuality. In *The fusion of psychiatry and science* (pp. 198–226). New York: Norton.

Sulloway, F. (1979). *Freud, biologist of the mind: Beyond the psychoanalytic legend*. New York: Basic Books.

Summers, F. (2008). Theoretical insularity and the crisis of psychoanalysis. *Psychoanalytic Psychology*, 25, 413–424.

——(2013a). Psychoanalysis in the age of "just do it." Presidential address to the APA Division 39 Spring Conference in Boston.

——(2013b). *The psychoanalytic vision: The experiencing subject, transcendence, and the therapeutic process*. New York: Routledge.

Szasz, T. (1961). *The myth of mental illness: Foundations of a theory of personal conduct*. New York: Harper & Row.

Tarnas, R. (1991). *Passion of the Western mind: Understanding the ideas that have shaped our world views*. New York: Harmony.

——(2006). *Cosmos and psyche*. New York: Viking.

——(2012). Notes on archetypal dynamics and complex causality. *Archai: The Journal of Archetypal Cosmology*, 4, 39–60.

Tarnas, R., Laszlo, E., Gablik, S., & Perez-Christi, A. (2001). The cosmic world – How we participate in thee and thou in us. *ReVision*, 23. 3, 42–48.

Taub, G. (2009). A confusion of tongues between psychoanalysis and philosophy: Is the controversy over drive versus relational theory a philosophical one? *International Journal of Psycho-Analysis*, 90, 507–527.

Tauber, A.I. (2009). Freud's dreams of reason: the Kantian structure of psychoanalysis. *History of the Human Sciences*, 22. 4, 1–29.

Taylor, C. (1985). *Philosophical papers: Volume 1, human agency and language*. Cambridge, UK: Cambridge University Press.

Taylor, E. (1999). *Shadow culture: Psychology and spirituality in America*. Washington, DC: Counterpoint Press.

——(2009). *The mystery of personality: A history of psychodynamic theories*. New York: Springer.

Tennes, M. (2007). Beyond intersubjectivity. *Contemporary Psychoanalysis*, 43, 505–525.

Torok, M. (1975/1994) Story of fear: The symptoms of phobia – the return of the repressed or the return of the phantom? In N. Abraham, & M. Torok (1994) *The shell and the kernel* (N.T. Rand, Ed. & Trans.). Chicago & London: University of Chicago Press.

Trilling, L. (1982), *Sincerity and authenticity*. Cambridge, MA: Harvard University Press.

Varela, F.J., Thompson, E., & Rosch, E. (1991). *The embodied mind: Cognitive and human experience*. Cambridge, MA: MIT Press.

von Franz, M.L. (2001). *Psyche and matter*. Boston, MA: Shambhala.

Wachtel, P. (2007). *Relational theory and the practice of psychotherapy*. New York: The Guilford Press.

——(2002). Probing the boundaries of the relational paradigm. *Psychoanalytic Dialogues*, 12, 207–225.

Watts, A. (2006). *Eastern wisdom, modern life: Collected talks: 1960–1969*. Novato, CA: New World Library.

Webster, J. (2011). *The life and death of psychoanalysis: On unconscious desire and its sublimation*. London: Karnac Books.

Whitaker, R. (2010). *Mad in America*. New York: Basic Books.

Whitehead, A.N. (1926). *Religion in the making: Lowell lectures, 1926*. New York: The Macmillan Company.

Wilber, K. (2000). *Integral psychology: Consciousness, spirit, psychology, therapy*. Boston, MA: Shambhala.

Winnicott, D.W. (1960). Ego distortion in terms of true and false self. In *The maturational pro- cesses and the facilitating environment: Studies in the theory of emotional development* (pp. 140–157). New York: International Universities Press.

——(1963a). From dependence towards independence in the development of the individual. In *The maturational processes and the facilitating environment: Studies in the theory of emotional development* (pp. 83–92). New York: International Universities Press.

——(1963b). Communicating and not communicating leading to a study of certain opposites. In *The maturational processes and the facilitating environment: Studies in the theory of emotional development* (pp. 179–192). New York: International Universities Press.

——(1966). Psycho-somatic illness in its positive and negative aspects. *International Journal of Psychoanalysis*, 47, 510–516.

——(1971). *Playing and reality*. New York: Basic Books.

Woolf, V. (1938). *Three guineas*. London: Hogarth Press.

Wright, B. (Director). (2004). *Manufacturing reality: Slavoj Žižek and the reality of the virtual*. Chicago: Olive Films.

Wyschogrod, E., Crownfield, D., & Raschke, C.A. (Eds) (1989). *Lacan and theological discourse*. Albany, NY: State University of New York Press.

Young-Eisendrath, P., & Hall, J. (1991). *Jung's self psychology: A constructivist perspective*. New York: The Guilford Press.

Zepf, S., Hartmann, S., & Zepf, F.D. (2007). Constructivism in psychoanalysis. *Canadian Journal of Psychoanalysis*, 15, 3–21.

Žižek, S. (2001). The one measure of true love is: you can insult the other. Spiked, November 15, downloaded from http://www.spiked-online.com/Articles/00000002D2C4.htm

——(2007). *How to read Lacan*. New York: Norton.

——(2007). *The indivisible remainder: On Schelling and related matters*. London; New York: Verso.

——(2009). *The sublime object of ideology* (2nd edition). New York: Verso.

INDEX